Crip Negativity

(Continued on page 91)

Crip Negativity

J. Logan Smilges

University of Minnesota Press
MINNEAPOLIS
LONDON

Excerpts from Travis Chi Wing Lau, "Pithy," in *Paring* (Georgetown, Ky.: Finishing Line Press, 2020), published with permission of the poet. Excerpts from Cameron Awkward-Rich, "Essay on the Awkward / Black / Object," in *Sympathetic Little Monster* (Los Angeles: Ricochet Editions, 2016), published with permission of the poet.

ISBN 978-1-5179-1558-2 (pb)
ISBN 978-1-4529-6959-6 (Ebook)
ISBN 978-1-4529-6960-2 (Manifold)

Published by the University of Minnesota Press, 2023
111 Third Avenue South, Suite 290
Minneapolis, MN 55401-2520
www.upress.umn.edu

Available as a Manifold edition at manifold.umn.edu

The University of Minnesota is an equal-opportunity educator and employer.

To all of my crip kin, disabled and not, who have given me permission to cripply feel my bad crip feelings. By assisting me into the shared pool of our negativity, you've helped me to recognize that I am never alone and that the work of dreaming is never complete.

Contents

1. Crip Negativity

MY NICKNAME IN HIGH school was Awkward John. I earned it because my name was John, and I was very awkward. Prior to high school, I had been homeschooled with my siblings in relative isolation, including several formative years on a farm about an hour outside of suburbia. The lack of contact with children my own age, paired with my readily apparent gender nonconformance, closeted homosexuality, and what I later came to recognize as a grab bag of mental disabilities, left me with few normatively developed social skills.

I walked too fast and carried a backpack too full. I sat so straight at my desk that my back never touched the chair. I demanded to be in the front row of every classroom in a seat that faced the door. I reminded teachers about homework. I attempted to spark impromptu political debates with classmates between sets of pushups at lunch. I asked out girls, who usually turned me down. And I held the hands of those poor few who agreed so tightly that our fingers would cramp. I was a theater kid but could not act, sing, or dance. I lifted weights with the football players but would cover my ears and run from the weight room if the volume of the stereo was turned too loud. Once, when a couple of boys were shooting spitballs at me during study hall, I slammed a textbook on their table. "The next time you hit me," I said, gulping back tears, "I will fucking ruin you." I then immediately went to the bathroom and cried.

And then, of course, there was the hug incident.

On my way to class one day, I noticed an acquaintance walking toward me, smile beaming, with his arms outstretched. I assumed he was coming in for a hug and, thrilled at the opportunity for friendly physical contact, I opened my arms in return. As it turns out, I was right about this person wanting a hug, but I was wrong about whom he wanted it from. I didn't know that his girlfriend was walking a few paces behind me. Realizing my misunderstanding a moment too late, the person juked right as my arms were closing in around him. I lost my balance, stumbled sideways, and swung my hand directly into a brick wall. There was an audible *crack* when my bones made contact. I remember looking, dazed, for a moment at my palm before everything went black.

I woke up in the nurse's office, where I learned that I had passed out, fallen backward over my backpack like a capsized turtle, and hit my head on the floor. Apparently unbothered by the sound of my breaking bones, my fall, or my unconsciousness, no student stopped to tend to me. The nurse found me deserted in the hallway on her way back from lunch and, with the help of the gym teacher, carried me to her office to wait for the paramedics. To this day, it is one of my most embarrassing memories and also perhaps the most representative of my time in high school. So many misunderstandings. So many missed cues. So many moments I knew I was being made fun of or outright mocked, even as I pretended I was unaware. So many times I could recognize my difference from the shape of others' faces. So many times I could feel their eyes glossing my awkwardness.

Thinking back on my time in high school, I am struck by the palpable anger I continue to hold toward my experience. Some of me wants to let the memories go as unoriginal bullying. Kids being kids. Perhaps this is true in part; sometimes kids (much like adults) are just mean for no reason. But another part of me is inclined to believe that there was something else going on—something more structural at play that warrants my ongoing anger. After all, there's always a reason some kids get bullied over others. Some differences seem to matter more, and the differential mattering of those differences matters. The disability studies scholar in me wants to call the differential mattering of my difference *ableism,* as a way to capture the disciplining of my enminded departure from neurotypicality. While some of my classmates were equal opportunity bullies, destroying the self-confidence of everyone they encountered, this group was in a decided minority. The virality of my nickname—Awkward John—read against my apparent invisibility (i.e., left alone and unconscious in a hallway) would suggest that much of the bullying I encountered was less a result of random injury than an effect of people's shared anxiety over my neuroqueerness.

The circulation of my nickname functioned as my classmates' meager attempt to safeguard the normativity of their own ways of thinking, moving, and feeling. My awkwardness needed to be policed because, if left unchecked, it risked exposing the fragility of normativity more broadly. If my queerness and disabilities were not suitably stigmatized, if I were not reminded daily of my social failures, it would become far more difficult for others to avoid justifying the more intense forms of discrimination and segregation faced by other students, such as disabled students restricted to "special ed" classrooms or poor and racialized students who, because of redlining and gerrymandering, were literally bussed to other schools. In a lot of ways, Awkward John had very little to do with me and far more to do with shoring up the boundaries of white cisheteroabledness against the threat of differences perceived as far greater than mine. If I could be sufficiently abjected, so too could others.

Here is where things start to get a little more complicated. The field of disability studies and the wider terrain of disability activism often frame ableism as a collection of access problems. If a person can't enter a room because there is no ramp, if they can't participate in a conversation because there is no sign language interpreter, or if they can't understand a contract because it is too full of unnecessary jargon, then that room, conversation, and contract are inaccessible. Inaccessibility occurs when disabled people and our needs are intentionally dismissed or accidentally overlooked. Either way, ableism is at work, barring disabled people from full participation.

But as my high school experience demonstrates, ableism casts a wider net than the language of access is able to capture. In my case, nothing about my education was inaccessible. I could get into the building and to all of my classes. I could understand the lessons and complete the assignments. I had a range of extracurricular activities I could choose from and participate in if I wanted. I had teachers who offered a variety of formal and informal accommodations to help me fulfill course objectives. And yet despite all this access, ableism still managed to make my life absolutely fucking miserable. If anything, I wanted *less* access, less contact with ableds, less time spent in spaces structured by neurotypicality, and less energy expended accommodating me into a community that exploited my neuroqueerness as an opportunity to ossify its superiority. Access didn't eliminate ableism; it enabled ableism to bare its teeth.

This book is about the ableism of access; or, rather, how too concerted a focus on individuals' access needs distracts from the messier, meaner, and more systemic ways that ableism operates in our world. Disability justice activist Mia Mingus writes that "access for the sake of access is not necessarily liberatory" (2017). In fact, access sometimes does little more than "reinforc[e] the status quo." In the American education system, the benchmark for accessibility is what's known as LRE or the "least restrictive environment." As part of the Individuals with Disabilities Education Act (IDEA), which guarantees all children "a free appropriate public education," Section 300.114 requires that "to the maximum extent appropriate, children with disabilities . . . are educated with children who are nondisabled." In an attempt to minimize segregation, LRE stipulates that, as much as possible, disabled students should use the same classrooms, teachers, and curricula as their nondisabled peers. Access, in this case, is synonymous with integration. The more thoroughly that disabled students are integrated into the world of ableds, the more "appropriate" their education must be—or so IDEA assumes. But this version of accommodation, what I call *integrative access*, fails to account for how ability operates as a structural norm, informing the ableist cultures into which disabled students are expected to integrate. My experience in high school was deeply shaped by ableism, even though I had all the access I needed for a successful integration. My education was "appropriate," in accordance with IDEA, but the conditions under which my education took place made it nearly unbearable. Moreover, the access extended to me via integration worked to further legitimize the disenfranchisement of other disabled and differently marginalized students.

I am left wondering, then, about the political utility of access. Does the language of inaccessibility name the violence we think it does? And does the energy we spend demanding access secure the kind of liberation we want it to? These questions are best understood within the context of the emerging field of "critical access studies," coined by Aimi Hamraie, that "challenges the treatment of access as a 'self-evident good'" (2017, 13). This field does not deny the importance of access, but it does interrogate "the discourses surrounding access" (269), prompting us to consider "access-knowledge" as a situated and relational epistemology rather than a given and objective account of the world (5). If we're going to talk about access, especially in universal terms, Hamraie reminds us that we have to ask ourselves, "Who *counts* as everyone and how can we *know*?" (5). This book builds on these questions to ask, further, *What* do we want access to, and *why* do we want access to it? I propose that access-knowledge is not only an epistemic object, per Hamraie, but also an ethical one. How we define access, deploy our access-knowledge, and direct our interests in accessibility all deserve critical attention.

There's no question that we are living in a world plagued by access problems, wherein disabled, poor, old, racialized, colonized, trans and gender nonconforming, and queer people are frequently left without the basic essentials they need to survive, let alone the equity they need to flourish. It remains the case, for instance, that many poor and racialized children, with and without disabilities, are denied access to a complete education. Statistically, students of color are both more likely than their white peers to be diagnosed with disabilities and less likely than their white peers to receive special education services (Erevelles and Minear 2010). I do not intend to downplay the classed and raced realities of inaccessibility in the U.S. education system or to cast doubt on the urgency with which we should be working toward greater access to better education for all. What I'm really after is not the availability of access but rather the outcome of access: What are we hoping access will do for us? What is the benefit of securing access to an education that purposefully misrepresents our country's legacy of settler-colonialism and slavery (Lopez 2021)? Whom does it serve to demand access to an education that includes only cisheterosex within its sexual health curriculum (Hubbard 2021)? How is life improved for disabled students if access to an education means suffering the brutality of having their disabilities exploited to protect the integrity of their abled peers' own insecurities?

Similar questions could be asked about the utility of access in other domains of life outside of education. In terms of labor, for instance, what is the value of access to employment when disabled people are one of the only adult populations who can legally be paid less than minimum wage (Selyukh 2020), when earning minimum wage is not enough to clear the poverty line, or when the working conditions at a job are so deplorable that they exacerbate existing disabilities or produce new ones? Regarding healthcare, how can we celebrate access to a medical industry that is built on knowledge gleaned from nonconsensual violence against enslaved Black women (Owens 2018), profits off people's dependence on insulin to survive (Sainato 2020), and enforces sex dimorphism on children born with intersex conditions (Malatino 2019)? Or, in what way do we even make sense of increased efforts to enhance the accessibility of prisons when the prison industrial complex presents one of the greatest threats to many marginalized communities, especially people of color and disabled people (Weill-Greenberg 2021; Ben-Moshe 2020)?

In all of these examples, access might offer a form of inclusion, perhaps even a necessary form, but it is an inclusion bereft of history, as well as the ways this history continues to shape our material present. As Mingus explains, access that can be reduced to integration does nothing "to transform the conditions that created inaccessibility in the first place" (2017). These are conditions that structure the very institutions and systems into which we have been demanding access. Institutions and systems such as public education, the workforce, the field of medicine, and the law were not merely made to serve abled people best; they were built on the explicit disavowal of disability. The humanist project that emerged during the Enlightenment era exalts the nondisabled bodymind as an essential characteristic of white supremacy, leading Dennis Tyler to conclude that "disability is central, not peripheral, to racial formation" in the United States (2022, 5). Mental disability, in particular, has been historically indicted as a moral failure, representing stunted development, rotted genes, and a threat to the evolutionary trajectory of humankind.

Along with cisheterosexuality, ability functions as a central pillar of whiteness and thus lies at the core of what it means to be a proper citizen and a productive consumer in the West. No amount of integration can undo the violence woven into the threads of the world as we know it. No number of open doors can air out the toxicity that stinks up the room. Access does not by itself fix ableism. To suggest or imply otherwise is to fall prey to a "cruel optimism" that can only end in disappointment when the access we demand merely shifts the variety of ableism we face (Berlant 2011). That is to say: Even if we get them to let us in, we can't make them want us there. Even if they say they want us there now, how do we trust them after all this time?

Perhaps, like me, you ask yourself some variation of this question frequently. And perhaps, also like me, the answer leaves you feeling pretty bad. It can be difficult to feel hopeful, desirable, or loved when—even after you've been given access—you're still left feeling all alone. Loneliness is unpleasant for everyone, but it takes on especial horror for disabled people who live so much of our lives in isolation. Unless you have experienced it yourself, it's hard to understand fully the ache of watching others live their lives while it feels as though you are merely aging. It's not the fear of missing out; it's just missing out. Day after day, season after season, year after year of not being healthy enough, not being strong enough, not being smart enough, not being attractive enough, not being happy enough, not being enough of anything to be enough. So when you finally secure access to something for the first time—maybe a concert, a graduate program, a job, a relationship, a surgery—and you realize that you are still feeling all alone, and that no one seems to care . . . well, devastating doesn't begin to cover it.

I don't know a single disabled person who hasn't at some point felt, however ephemerally or fleetingly, that they aren't, in the end, a burden. Because if we were anything else, so it seems, we wouldn't be so alone. *Life would be easier; no, life would be possible,* we think to ourselves. *We could live if the world wanted us. But it doesn't want us. We aren't wanted. We are lonely because we are alone, and we are alone because we are truly and utterly unwanted.*

Defining Crip Negativity

The remainder of this book is about where lonely people go from here, from that feeling of stultifying isolation. *Crip negativity* is the phrase I use to describe bad crip feelings felt cripply. It refers, on one hand, to the many bad feelings that disabled, debilitated, and otherwise nonnormatively embodyminded people encounter with some regularity: pain, guilt, shame, embarrassment, exhaustion, fear, and anger, to name just a few. On another hand, crip negativity names how these bad feelings are felt: deeply, slowly, tearfully, fitfully, sleeplessly, suicidally, hungrily, among the long list of excessive and pathological ways that crips feel (Forrest 2020). On a third hand (because there's no reason people should only have two hands), crip negativity captures a growing, gnawing skepticism I feel toward the language of access and the category of disability.

For some people, a version of this skepticism will not be particularly new or original. Disability activists and disability studies scholars have long troubled the stability of *disability* as it is typically defined by the medical industrial complex. *Disability* is not a simple fact of the world, we say, but a carefully curated and culturally contingent idea about bodyminds and difference. Enviable and marketable differences are propped up as characteristics of "diversity," whereas less desirable or less economically profitable differences have been historically relegated to the status of a disability. What makes crip negativity unique is that its pessimism is directed not at the definition of disability, per se, but at the function of *disability* as a category of being. That is, much as I am less critical of access's availability than I am of access's utility, I am also less interested in what counts as a disability than I am in why it matters: What does the category of *disability* do? And for whom?

Crip negativity proposes that the category of *disability* functions primarily as a regulatory mechanism by which humanity can be distributed and withheld. Whether articulated within medical, social, or political frameworks, *disability* operates as a plasticizing ontology, infusing individuals and populations with varying degrees and qualities of humanness based on their proximity to normativity. Of particular concern to me is the way normativity is structured by whiteness and cisheteronormativity, along with abledness—all mutually entwined and contingent vectors of power that glean their meaning by manufacturing opposition in the forms of disability, gender nonconformance, sexual deviance, and racial difference. Charged by overlapping and at times conflicting strains of negativity in queer studies, Black studies, and crip theory, I am intrigued by how the category of *disability* operates not only as a marker of abjection or marginalization but also as an invitation for subjectification.

By subjectification, I am thinking alongside transnational and feminist scholars of disability, such as Nirmala Erevelles, Janet Jakobsen, Christina Crosby, and Jasbir Puar, who all work to expose disability in its "global context" (Erevelles 2011). This context reveals that disability not only takes different shapes across cultures and history but also that these differing shapes contribute to the stratification of care and access, that is, "where the emancipation of some bodies is related to the disposability of other bodies" (Erevelles 2014). Jakobsen and Crosby propose the useful "geopolitical model of disability" (2020, 78) to dial in on how disability identity and the language of access in the West can obfuscate or intensify forms of debilitation that harm people on the other side of the planet and in nearby communities who are never recognized as disabled. Civilian casualties of war, care workers, factory laborers, and survivors of police violence are all populations whose experiences of pain and injury can be exacerbated by the exceptionalization of the Western disabled subject. "The stigmatization of disability as deficit justifies the right to maim" explains Puar. "The production of widespread debilitation is key to maintaining colonial rule" (2017, 161). The category of *disability* can, all at once, signal a person's struggle against ableism, reinforce boundaries around the definition of disability as contoured by Western medicine, implicitly authorize imperial violence by alleging a state's mistreatment of disabled people, and capitalize on the effects of that violence to further entrench colonial authority.

It is worth reiterating that crip negativity is not merely opposed to a particular model of disability; rather, it is a staunch critique of the category of *disability* in all its medical, social, and political variations. The problem with *disability*, much like the problem with access, is not definitional but structural. *Disability* gleans its rhetorical power from specific historical, cultural, and geographic contexts, and these contexts pervade all frameworks for understanding *disability*—no matter how conservative or progressive. On the conservative end, the medical model defines *disability* as a problem with the body or mind that demands rehabilitation, management, or cure. Missing from this definition is an awareness that the criteria defining "problematic" bodies or minds have varied throughout history and across cultures. More progressive models of disability, such as the social model (Shakespeare 2006), the cultural model (Snyder and Mitchell 2005), and the political/relational model (Kafer 2013), have attempted to counter the medical model by troubling the naturalness of *disability* or by revealing the category's political potentialities. But I fear that even these progressive frameworks either smuggle in the organizing logics of the medical model, and thus bar sociocultural contextualization, or they attempt to account for that context by emptying *disability* of the conditions surrounding its own emergence. In both cases, *disability* is fantasized as a recuperable object, one that can be endlessly repurposed without fully reconciling how it came to be in the first place.

The social model, for example, promotes the idea that *disability* is a product of the built environment, that disability is not reducible to "flaws" in an individual's body or mind but is produced by the "misfit" between an individual's impairments and an environment that was not designed for them (Garland-Thomson 2011). While this model does an excellent job of interrogating the individualizing impulse of the medical model, it does little to contest the criteria by which we recognize an impairment as an impairment. In other words, the social model interrogates the cause of disability phenomenology but not the assumption of a stable disability ontology, leaving unchecked the medical model's implicit assertion that *disabled*, as a subject position, is primordial.

Other progressive models of disability are more critical of *disability*'s ontological status, but their attempts to salvage the category remain suspicious. For example, Sharon Snyder and David Mitchell's "cultural model of disability" effectively identifies the reciprocal relationship between "therapeutic beliefs about disability and disabled people's experiences" (2005, 7). They recognize that who disabled people understand themselves to be, including their identification as disabled, is informed by the medical model, even if that model is disavowed. "Impairment," Snyder and Mitchell explain, "is both human variation encountering environmental obstacles *and* socially mediated difference that lends group identity and phenomenological perspective" (10). *Disability*, in this sense, can never be fully disentangled from the medical model because that model has already delimited our terms of engagement.

Alison Kafer addresses this frustrating tether by turning it into a political opportunity. Her political/relational model of *disability* "recognizes the difficulty in determining who is included in the term 'disabled,' refusing any assumption that it refers to a discrete group of particular people with certain similar essential qualities" (2013, 10). For Kafer, *disability*'s politics emerge from its inherent instability and from the idea that it, much like *queer* in queer studies, is forever "open to dissent and debate" (9). It's because of this instability, rather than in spite of it, Kafer argues, that the category of *disability* can be capacious and flexible beyond the boundaries of the medical industrial complex. As much as I appreciate Snyder and Mitchell's cross-cultural sensitivity and share in Kafer's optimism for *disability*'s queer volatility, I am wary of the sleight of hand that attempts to reconcile *disability*'s ontological violence without engaging the specific conditions that gave rise to the reclamation of *disability* itself.

It's not my purpose in this book to rehearse the entire cultural history of *disability*, but it seems prudent to acknowledge that the originary context for *disability*'s sociopolitical turn is relevant to its ongoing political life. In much the same way that queer studies scholars have recently started to name *queer*'s intellectual history beginning in the 1990s by unpacking the effect of that history on the formation of the field, I am curious about the extent to which *disability*'s liberatory uptake also requires genealogical attention. In *Disturbing Attachments,* Kadji Amin argues that *queer*'s mobility is a siren in the waters of critique: scholars fail to notice what *queer* excludes because they are tempted by the term's seemingly infinite expansiveness. *Queer*'s appetite appears to be endless, but Amin reminds us that it's not. Like all terms, *queer* is selective. As I've written elsewhere, with every attachment *queer* forms, a "disattachment" rises in its wake (Smilges 2022). Amin suggests that much of the problem lies in *queer*'s sublated disciplinary history:

> Forgetting this history is useful to the field precisely because it permits us to refuse to define or to historicize *queer,* to say we are holding it open to indefinite becomings, all the while making implicit and explicit arguments that draw both their conviction and their appeal from *queer*'s affective charge, that is, from its disavowed historicity. (184)

Queer only seems expansive to the extent we choose to believe it is, to the extent we allow ourselves to feel that it is. We cling tightly to the fantasy of *queer*'s mobility because it feels good to believe in something. It's nice to feel like we can count on an idea to do everything we hope it will, for once.

I worry, though, that a variation of the "affective charge" driving *queer*'s colonial impulse emanates also from *disability,* stemming from a series of racial and class tensions that developed during the early years of the disability rights movement in the United States. Despite their attempt to forge solidarity across differently disabled people, many disability rights activists struggled to make room for people's differences beyond their disabilities. Issues of race and class, especially, were often jettisoned due to fear that they would dilute the potency of a unified disability identity. Jennifer L. Erkulwater explains that throughout the 1970s, leading disability activists articulated their agenda primarily in terms of "consumer control and self-help," which contradicted the efforts of labor organizers and Black activists who were more critical of capitalism and rhetorics of independence (2018, 383; Schalk 2022). Despite pushback from Black disabled people, such as Johnnie Lacy and Donald Galloway who attempted to diversify the movement's goals, employment and independent living remained the primary foci of mainstream disability organizing until the 1990s (Lukin 2013).

In order to secure government funding for these objectives, leaders of the disability rights movement, who "were mostly white and much more educated than the typical person with a disability," worked to isolate the category of *disability* from other lines of marginalization (Erkulwater 2018, 380). Disabled people needed to appear as a coherent group, they argued, even if that meant downplaying the needs of multiply marginalized disabled people. While employment and independent living were (and remain) important metrics for civic participation, they did little to challenge the extractive logics under capitalism that equate an individual's value with their capacity to produce and, by extension, to consume. As Marta Russell and Ravi Malhotra explain, "A strategy of disability liberation politics entirely dependent on . . . purchasing power is so impoverished as to be of assistance to only a tiny fraction of the most privileged disabled people" (2009). Unless paired with additional, more radical goals, employment and independent living end up reinforcing the liberalism linking economic productivity, independence, and citizenship.

The disability rights movement's concerted effort to rehabilitate the economic potential of disabled people resulted in a rather conservative political agenda. While more radical disability activism certainly existed alongside the conservatism of the mainstream disability rights movement, such as that carried out by the Black Panther Party and the National Black Women's Health Project, it often adopted vocabularies and forms of expression that were illegible under the rubric of *disability* (Schalk 2022). Nevertheless, it has been suggested that the disability rights movement was a necessary building block for more recent and intersectional efforts toward disability justice. "Disabled citizenship and disabled world-making," Ruth Osorio proposes, "share a complicated and interconnected legacy, illustrating the need for multiple forms of belonging in the pursuit of disabled liberation" (2022, 249). For Osorio, the disability rights movement helped to catalyze "a new era" for disability politics that could afford to be more critical of the forms of integrative access sought out by earlier generations (259). As a benefactor of these earlier generations' efforts, I feel torn between gratitude for the life I have and frustrated by the compromises that made it possible. I don't want to appear ungenerous toward the legacies of our disabled elders and ancestors, but I do want to be accountable for our community's history, including the history of those whose needs were de-prioritized. Anti-ableism requires mutual commitments to anti-racism and anti-capitalism because disability, race, and class are categorically and phenomenologically entwined.

Among the most pressing examples of this triangulation is the welfare system. As Jina Kim argues, "Ableist reasoning anchors antiwelfare rhetoric" (2021, 80). Even if not all disabled people are in need of welfare, it remains the case that "the language of disability undergirds the ongoing erosion of public resources" (82). Both the experience of poverty and the racialized figuration of impoverishment are disability issues, in no small part because Black and Indigenous people are more likely to experience disability than all other racial groups (Courtney-Long et al. 2016). By centering economic rehabilitation and neglecting to prioritize the uneven economic conditions facing multiply marginalized disabled people, the disability rights movement catered to those who already had access to a number of privileged resources. Moreover, by refusing to organize from the margins of the disability community, the movement ultimately contributed to the forms of racialized ableism that disproportionately harm poor disabled and disabled people of color. It was a political strategy geared toward integrative access: prioritizing the realignment of disabled people with existing institutional and economic norms over challenging the society that created them.

The unique needs of disabled people of color and those without advanced degrees were dismissed in favor of an agenda that universalized the category of *disability* by sublimating its contingencies with race and class. Economic rehabilitation appeared possible only because it had been thoroughly deracinated. Whiteness and wealth, through their unspoken centrality, structured the emergence of the disability rights movement, effectively laying the groundwork for a field of disability studies that itself depends on whiteness "as its constitutive underpinning" (Bell 2006, 275). The historical conditions surrounding the early years of disability activism and informing the birth of disability studies lead me to wonder about the implicit assumptions guiding *disability* as a reclaimed and explicitly politicized category. Is it possible, for instance, that the expansiveness of *disability*—not unlike *queer*'s mobility—risks a kind of rhetorical negligence through its implicit disavowal of the category's own historicity? What does *disability* continue to exclude when we use it to cover so much ground? Whose lives does it obfuscate? What does *disability* leave unnamed when it claims to name so much?

Perhaps predicting these sorts of questions, Kafer proposes a "critical reading" practice that simultaneously "trace[s] the ways in which [disabled people] have been forged as a group" and "the ways in which those forgings have been incomplete, or contested, or refused" (2013, 12). Critical reading, in this case, is a method of accountability in line with the one I mention above, prompting us to consider not only what disability *is* or how it *means* but also how it has *emerged* as a category of analysis. Kafer suggests that *disability* might be understood "less as diagnostic category and more as collective affinity" (12–13). *Disability* not as who I am but who I am with. Sami Schalk (2017) mobilizes this definition as "(dis)ability," where the parenthetical captures "a system of social norms" that includes those regulating gender, sexuality, race, and class, along with disability. To theorize *disability* collectively is also to think intersectionally. It is difficult to find fault with this intrinsically relational approach. Who can deny the charm of intersectional, collective affinity? If we agree on *disability* as a node through which new relations can be formed, regardless of diagnostic status, there will always be opportunities for revision on whom the category can name and what work it can do.

It's for this reason that I am persuaded by Robert McRuer's *Crip Theory* (2006), which channels the political urgency of *queer* into *disability*'s unique phenomenology. The "crip" in crip negativity comes from my confidence that, regardless of the language we use to describe it, there is something powerful about embodyminded difference. As McRuer says, "It is not the term itself that is crucial"— whether we use the language of disability or not—"but whether or not, or how, it might affect or effect certain desirable futures" (2006, 41). Kafer and McRuer both believe in disability, no matter what we call it, as an embodyminded force that, through the maintenance of its existence, through the care we give to sustain disabled lives, can contest the ableism that structures our collective present. I join them in this belief, and my tender heart yearns for the hope they bear toward the future.

But if I'm being honest with myself and with you, I have some lingering doubts. These doubts emerge from my skepticism over the realities of building collective affinity in the context of *disability*, a category that cannot be easily emptied of its pathological origins or neatly disarticulated from its steady march toward liberal subjectification. As much as I like the premise of redefining *disability* in terms of affinity, I cannot help but to worry that the terms will always be haunted by the conflicting strands of *disability*'s diagnostic past and increasingly liberal present. In the first case, I'm not sure how to get away from the irony driving *disability*'s internal grammar: that there is no disability without diagnosis, no diagnosis without symptomatology, and no symptomatology without able-normativity. Even with the rise of self-diagnosis in Mad and neurodivergent communities, disability identity remains haunted by Western medicine, out of which many of the racist and cisheterosexist criteria for diagnoses were developed. It's for this reason that Calvin Warren (2018) and Therí Alyce Pickens (2019) both argue that in an antiblack world, insanity and madness are requisite conditions of Blackness. In the second case, *disability* can no longer be regarded as always already marginal. Sometimes it's not-so-marginal. Sometimes, as the flourishing mental health industrial complex indicates, it's even pretty damn close to normative. How do we establish and sustain affinity for the purpose of liberation around a category that flirts with normative?

Admittedly, pivoting away from *disability* and toward *crip,* as Kafer and McRuer propose, offers a tempting opportunity to short-circuit *disability*'s structural problems. Claiming *crip* allows disabled and nondisabled people alike to "acknowledg[e] that we all have bodies and minds with shifting abilities, and [to wrestle] with the political meanings and histories of such shifts" (Kafer 2013, 13). *Crip* invites us to think with Schalk's (dis)ability, positioning ourselves not within an abled/disabled binary but within a "wider social system" (2018, 6). The cross-movement and coalitional potentials of *crip* are promising. *Crip* can do good work, and I have no beef with it. But we cannot make the same mistakes with *crip* as we did with *queer* and as we are currently making with *disability;* we cannot convince ourselves that *crip* has no history, no disciplinary context, no conditions of emergence. Shifting toward *crip* does not solve *disability*'s ontological crisis. *Crip* cannot fix what's broken with *disability*—and I use the language of brokenness intentionally—because *crip* is a descendant of the politics that broke *disability*. While *crip* does not share *disability*'s same pathological origin or necessarily its trajectory of recuperation into a respectable subject position, it was nevertheless born out of a discrete set of affective conditions in response to *disability,* its origins, and its recuperation.

Disability structured the emergence of *crip,* so it should come as no surprise that *crip* feels a lot like *disability*. Despite the fact that Carrie Sandahl originally theorized "cripping" as a critical practice meant to "expose the arbitrary delineation between normal and defective," the word often appears in its nominal form to indicate an identity to be claimed or a position to be held (2003, 37). There's nothing wrong with using *crip* in this way—Schalk (2013) proposes that its identitarian form can "work both with and against identity"—but its prevalence underscores people's desire to maintain *crip*'s linguistic kinship with the category of *disability*. We are accustomed to *being* disabled, so it feels natural to *be* crip. But as Christina Cedillo and Remi Yergeau remind us, "Crip is a verb" (2019). *Crip* is meant to do something that *disability* cannot, and that something includes directly contesting the category of *disability* itself, especially its (neo)liberalization (McRuer 2006, 41). Too often is *crip* deployed as an extension of *disability,* a method of expanding the category to establish filiation with other identities, experiences, and locations. This work is important, but it cannot come at the expense of foregoing our responsibility to cripping *disability*.

I worry that, in the interest of preserving the integrity of *disability,* we are inclined to widen the category instead of to interrogate why it needs to be widened. In much the same way that we should be suspicious of spaces and institutions that belatedly offer us access, so too should we be wary of *disability*'s own legacy of inaccessibility. *Crip* can help us do this work if we let it. However, until *crip*'s critical valence achieves greater circulation, I remain ambivalent about its relationship to *disability,* just as I am ambivalent about *disability*'s relationship to normativity.

Cripping Negativity

Among my intentions with crip negativity is to reignite *crip,* not in such a way that disavows the affective conditions of its emergence but in order to direct *crip*'s critical gaze back at those conditions and at the category of *disability*. The "negativity" appended to *crip* serves two functions: one descriptive and one referential. In the first case, negativity heralds the bad feelings I mentioned above. Disabled people feel a lot of bad feelings, and crips like me are additionally weighed down by the bad feelings we bear toward the category of *disability*. The initial definition I offer for crip negativity—bad crip feelings felt cripply—sits in the tension between *disability* and *crip*. I am referring not only to those of us who wield *crip* to critique *disability* but also to those disabled folks who actively work against the interests of other disabled and marginalized people.

Consider, for example, Greg Abbott, the disabled, Republican governor of Texas. Since I began writing this book, Abbott has blamed wind turbines for widespread infrastructure failures that endangered thousands of lives during a winter storm (Shepherd 2021), instituted Operation Lone Star that legalizes the immediate imprisonment of all border-crossing immigrants without formal charges or legal aid (McCullough 2021), oversaw the recriminalization of abortion through a "trigger law" that went into effect after *Roe v. Wade* was overturned (Mekelburg 2022), ordered that parents who procure healthcare for their trans kids be investigated as child abusers (Dey and Harper 2022), presented virtually at a National Rifle Association meeting within days the Uvalde school shooting (Talbot, DiCasimirro, and Richards 2022), and been subject to a federal lawsuit brought on by fourteen disabled children over his prohibition of mask mandates (Caprariello and Falcon 2021). As if that were not enough, Abbott has also previously argued against state mandates to comply with the Americans with Disabilities Act and invoked "sovereign immunity claims" to defend the state of Texas against lawsuits by disabled people (*Dallas Morning News* 2014). This is the same man who has received nearly $8 million from a lawsuit he won over the accident that caused his own disability (*Dallas Morning News* 2014). The man is a menace, and he manipulates his own experience of disability to warrant state violence.

While Abbott may be rare in his position of power (though Madison Cawthorn, a former congressman from North Carolina, also comes to mind), there are many disabled people and abled allies who, despite their good intentions, wind up re-entrenching the forms of structural ableism that they claim to oppose. I'm thinking especially of when disabled politicians, celebrities, athletes, influencers, and even scholars sell out as inspiration porn, buy in to overcoming narratives, or attempt to frame themselves as existing at the pinnacle of oppression. The first group allows themselves to be exploited for abled catharsis; they milk the pathos that their disability elicits from people who get off on believing someone else's life is worse than theirs. The second group trades in the opportunity for community with other disabled people for the pursuit of abledness, of achieving or reclaiming a bodymind that is adaptable to the world as it is, including the ways it harms others. The final group clings to single-axis, identity-based logics that pit disabled people's access needs against all other communities and their needs, as if access is the sole property of disabled people, as if access friction isn't inevitable in all liberation struggles, and as if we aren't all trying to fight the same enemies.

How many more magazine covers do I need to see that feature thin, disabled white people bragging about their fitness achievements? How many more academic articles do I need to read that call for expanded access to inherently racist curricula or institutions? How many more times will I have to endure a debate on social media over whether a particular form of protest is ableist because it cannot accommodate everyone all at once? I'm getting bored, and I'm getting impatient.

These bad crip feelings expose the other, referential function of negativity. My original introduction to critical negativity occurred in the context of queer theory, an early iteration of queer studies that blossomed in the 1990s. Figures including Leo Bersani and Lee Edelman represented a wave of negativity that cast serious doubt on the viability of LGBT politics. With what has come to be known as the "antisocial thesis," these figures articulated a queer critique against the category of homosexuality for many of the same reasons that I am now troubled by the category of *disability* (Caserio et al. 2006). They worried that society had become so drenched in heteronormativity that there was simply no possible route to gay equality. The terms of society were tethered to heterosexuality in such a way that "resignification, or redeployment, or hyperbolic miming"—all the ways that gay activists had tried to articulate themselves as distinct from straight people—came up short because they were "too closely imbricated in the norms they continue[d]" (Bersani 1995, 51). Much like my frustration with efforts to secure integrative access, which seeks to accommodate disability instead of redressing the ableism that originally prohibited access, so too does the antisocial thesis launch an intracommunity interrogation of what queers really want. Is it assimilation or liberation? There cannot be both, these theorists argue, because liberation requires a total renunciation of society, a giving up of the social and its promises of qualified inclusion. "Without such a rejection," Bersani says, "social revolt is doomed to repeat the oppressive conditions that provoked the revolt" (172). It's only by disavowing the world we have that queers might begin to imagine the world anew.

The rhetorical force of the antisocial thesis comes to a head In Edelman's *No Future: Queer Theory and the Death Drive*. As the book's title provocatively suggests, Edelman argues that there can be no future for queers within the existing social order, which has come to be defined by "reproductive futurism" (2004, 2). Reproductive futurism refers to the compulsory nature of living in service of "the Child," of future generations, that is, imagining futurity in terms of heterosexual reproduction. Since cis homosexuals, who were the primary subject of Edelman's thinking, cannot reproduce on their own, they come to represent "the bar to every realization of futurity, the resistance, internal to the social, to every social structure or

form" (4). For him, queers are the necessary antagonists to reproductive futurism and, as such, will never be able to secure social
legitimacy. "Neither liberal inclusionism . . . nor the redemptive
hope of producing brave new social collectivities" Edelman warns,
"can escape the insistence of the antisocial in social organization"
(Caserio et al. 2006, 821). The antisocial thesis names negativity not
as *a* queer position but as *the* queer position. This dismal conclusion
leads Edelman to describe the trajectory of queer life in terms of
"the death drive," an unrelenting magnetism between queers and
everything the social is not (2004, 9).

Rather than continue a failed project of contesting our constitutive abjection, Edelman proposes that queers opt for an "embrace of
queer negativity"—one that does not attempt to invent an alternative
social order but, instead, rejects the social and futurity altogether,
effectively "dispossess[ing] the social order of the ground on which
it rests" (6). For Edelman, negativity is both the extant position
that the social order has forced queers to assume and an affective
anti-politic that leads to the social order's undoing. By altering how
we approach negativity, by rendering the death drive desirable, *No
Future* calls queers forth as the ultimate "advocates of abortion" and
as evangelizers of the bad news that "the future is mere repetition
and just as lethal as the past" (31). Queers need to stop trying to fix
the world, Edelman suggests, because the world is not broken. You
can't fix rotten.

Readers who are familiar with Edelman's polemic and with
the antisocial thesis will likely know that both have been widely
critiqued. As queer of color and disabled scholars point out, the
antisocial thesis depends on sweeping claims that, while energeti-
cally tempting (it's fun to vibe with), ignore important differences
between abled white gays and people who are differently marginalized. Jeff Nunokawa refers to this problem as *monism*, the pre-
sumption that society can be reduced to "a univocal entity" and
that all of us are "more or less indifferent instantiations . . . of this
entity" (2007, 558). It's easier to propose antisociality as the singular
solution to reproductive futurism when so much complexity is left

out of the equation, especially when that complexity includes lived experiences that you yourself have not had. The univocal entity implied by the antisocial thesis is a fantasy of oversimplified power dynamics dreamt up by a small group of white gay men who neglect to recognize the relative privilege of their perspective.

Instead of qualifying their claims by situating the plight of white gays alongside other struggles for liberation, this group purports to speak from "the View from Nowhere," which Courtney Bailey reads Susan Bordo to mean that their work "relies . . . on a closed system that feigns universality and casts material and personal experience as irrelevant to abstract theorizing" (2019). Both disability and race, alongside other axes of difference beyond sexuality, become moot points that distract from, rather than nuance, theories of the social. The antisocial thesis presents queerness as a deracinated, disembodied position, despite the whiteness and abledness that structure its conditions of possibility.

These racial and disability tensions take center stage in conversations about alternatives to *No Future*. Famously, José Esteban Muñoz and Kafer each position their oft-cited books in full or partial opposition to Edelman's work. While both scholars admire Edelman's dissatisfaction with the status quo, agreeing that reproductive futurism is a flawed and dangerous system of temporal governance, they take issue with Edelman's inattention to how different experiences within the existing social order necessarily affect the desirability of an antisocial position. Committing to queer negativity on Edelman's terms, argues Muñoz, "is imaginable only if one can frame queerness as a singular abstraction that can be subtracted and isolated from a larger social matrix" (2009, 94). Reproductive futurism presumes a Child that "is indeed always already white," despite the real, wanting, and sticky lives of children of color, poor children, queer and trans children, and disabled children for whom the future is rarely offered and never guaranteed (95).

Quite the opposite, these children are often "framed as sick, pathological, as contagious"—not only in biomedical terms but also as eugenic threats to the human species (Kafer 2013, 32). Kafer points out that what reproductive futurism ultimately lays bare is the entanglement of race, class, gender, and sexuality under the banner of disability: "The always already white Child is also always already healthy and nondisabled; disabled children are not part of this privileged imaginary except as the abject other" (33). What harms disabled children, as well as everyone deemed a threat to the health and wellness of society, is not futurity but the unimaginative futures for which we've allowed ourselves to settle. What we need is not no future but more futures, more choices, more ways of nourishing one another's dreams.

It is this expanded, thirsting look toward futurity that drives Muñoz's and Kafer's projects. Muñoz's "queer utopianism" explicitly invokes "not only relationality but also futurity" in order to call for "a renewed investment in social theory" (2009, 10). While he does not entirely disavow negativity, Muñoz channels it into a kind of perpetual dissatisfaction with the present, one that drives us not away from society but toward other, new societies on the "horizon" (19). Kafer, who thoroughly cites Muñoz, argues for "a politics of crip futurity" that pursues "an elsewhere—and, perhaps, an 'elsewhen'—in which disability is understood otherwise" (2013, 3). She, too, does not entirely turn away from negativity, readily acknowledging "how futurity has been the cause of much violence against disabled people" (31). Ultimately, though, she joins Muñoz in a more leveled critique that attempts to mine alternative futurities for what they might still have to offer those of us who were never promised a future to begin with. Sean Lee has called these alternative futurities, collectively, the "crip horizon," linking Muñoz and Kafer through their shared hope in "an ever moving future" (2019). It is a politics of futurity that requires, at the very least, a will to believe that a better future is possible, as well as the strength to keep trudging toward it.

The thrust of crip negativity lies between this will to believe and the strength needed to sustain it. I believe, along with Muñoz, Kafer, and Lee, in the possibility of a different future. I will myself into believing every day because without that will, I'm not sure I could keep myself alive. If I thought that there was no future *at all* for disabled people, well, I don't think I'd see much purpose in surviving the present. But I also acknowledge that some days I don't have the energy to think much about the future, let alone to pursue it. Some days my bad crip feelings are felt so cripply that I live in a heap of tears and blankets. Sometimes I feel despair—total, fucking despair. While a part of me is tempted to read these days and times as aberrations, temporary departures from the longer oeuvre of my affectivity that is, perhaps, less intensely pessimistic, I want to honor the depth of my bad crip feelings as no more or less aberrant than the bouts of optimism I feel at other times.

My thinking on time and feeling is informed by conversations in disability studies and Mad studies on how people's experiences of disability, trauma, and madness can contour their relationships to temporality. Ellen Samuels, for instance, tells us that "*crip time is grief time*" (2017). Clementine Morrigan offers "trauma time" as "a queer time traveling" produced by "dissociation, executive dysfunction, and confusion" (2017, 53, 56). And La Marr Jurelle Bruce adds "madtime" to name the "phenomenologies of madness," including "the quick time of mania; the slow time of depression; the infinite, exigent now of schizophrenia; and the spiraling now-then-now-then of melancholia" (2021, 32). Taken together, crip time, trauma time, and mad time capture the affectivity of temporality, the dimension of feeling with/in time and sensing time with/in feeling.

Sometimes I feel like queer and crip politics oriented toward the horizon or toward futurity don't let me sit long enough in my grief. My grief for my body and its scars, for my mind and its nightmares, for my parents and their fear, for my first love and his stolen youth, for my communities and the way we sharpen our pain, for our shared world and the weight of its history. Disabled people store so much grief in our bones; sometimes it holds us up and keeps us fighting, but other times it pulls us down, sealing us to the bed, bath, or silence. What I find so comforting about queer negativity is not its disavowal of the future but its capacity to pause in the present. Negativity gives me time to mourn. It lets me feel my bad crip feelings as cripply as I want and sometimes as cripply as I can: screaming into the void of pillows packed around my head, kicking and pounding the asphalt with my fists, or fucking my partner so hard that the pain melts me into an oblivion that feels like nothing. And it's there, in the crystalized moment of the scream, the pound, the fuck, that I can begin—not to imagine a future but to breathe myself out of the past.

It is with this appreciation for the way negativity holds open crip, trauma, and mad time that I find myself unable to part with Edelman, even as I acknowledge the flaws in his thinking. The antisocial thesis allows me to indulge my negativity without demanding justification or immediate political application. Sometimes I just want to be sad! I just want to be mad! I just want to be disappointed. My intention is not to reclaim the antisocial thesis so much as it is to expand it, to turn its negativity back on itself—that is, to add queer theory's embedded racism and ableism to the list of reasons I'm grieving. In some ways, I am parroting Muñoz's own methodological reasoning in *Cruising Utopia,* where he chooses to cite Martin Heidegger, a philosopher with debated Nazi sympathies, over other thinkers who are more frequently cited in queer studies. Muñoz writes, "Although I too have a great disdain for what Heidegger's writing became, I nonetheless look on it as a failure worth knowing, a potential that faltered but can be nonetheless reworked in the service of a different politics and understanding of the world" (2009, 16). *No Future* and the antisocial thesis are, for me, failures worth knowing. They offer errors to learn from, certainly, but they also offer a temporal structure in which that learning can occur. This structure, what I've been describing as a kind of dis/affective lag between the grief of the present and the hope of the future, might herald different futures altogether. Perhaps negativity needed to be disavowed in order for its value to be realized. Perhaps what the antisocial thesis offers, more than anything, is permission to be crippled by bad crip feelings, including those felt toward the model of anti-future futurism that the antisocial thesis offers.

Cripping Disability

Among the crippling bad crip feelings that the antisocial thesis allows me to name is my frustration with the category of *disability*, the way it, too, is increasingly being used to promise a kind of future that I don't want. This is a future geared not only toward reproduction, á la reproductive futurism, but also toward a form of rehabilitation that "fantasize[s] the eradication of disability" (Mollow 2012, 288). According to Anna Mollow, such "rehabilitative futurism" works alongside reproductive futurism to ensure the continuity of hetero-ablenormativity through the elimination of disability, whether by way of "a recovery of a crippled (or hobbled) economy, a cure for society's ills, [or] an end to suffering and disease" (288). Channeling the reflexive negativity described above, we might also understand rehabilitative futurism in terms of *disability*'s subjectification, its capacitation.

I am referring to forms of state and institutional recognition that interpellate *disability* into a respectable and perhaps even desirable subject position, one that can be invoked to justify the ongoing abjection of poor and racialized populations. This is a futurism marked not by the rehabilitation of disabled people into nondisabled people but by the rehabilitation of disabled people into proper citizens of the state: people granted rights and protection under antidiscrimination laws by a nation occupying the unceded lands of native and Indigenous tribes, built by enslaved peoples trafficked across the Atlantic, and sustained by a combination of extractive wage labor, stolen resources, a militarized police force, and a privatized prison system. Rehabilitation has never only been about altering the material bodymind; it's also been about revising what the bodymind means, how it signifies. Rehabilitative efforts to resignify the disabled bodymind work in concert with attempts to secure integrative access: both are more concerned about the facade of inclusivity than with the conditions of embodying alterity.

The more energy we expend rehabilitating the category of *disability* into the liberal state and the narrower our focus on access for the purpose of inclusivity, the more we inadvertently contribute to the "heteroperpetuity" of the liberal state itself (Bruce 2016). Thinking alongside Bruce's use of the term, I urge us to be cognizant of how *disability* can be instrumentalized alongside heteronormativity to propagate white supremacy and anti-Blackness, ultimately ossifying heteronorms and "produc[ing] material structures and conditions to sustain those heteronorms" (2016, 169). Historically, these material structures have included the pathologization of Black gender and sexual configurations—racism and ableism cooperating to elevate the desirability of white abledness and to ensure the disrepute of Black and disabled people. The subjectification of *disability* introduces a variation of heteroperpetuity (dis-perpetuity?) that welcomes *disability* into an adjacent relationship with normativity so long as it reifies the benevolence of white supremacy and the settler state.

Earlier in this chapter, when I offered a crip negative definition of *disability* as a *regulatory mechanism,* I was dialing in on the dialectic between *disability*'s history and its liberal future. There is no question that disability and experiences of disablement are often linked to marginalization, but it is also the case that marginalization experienced within the category of *disability* must be read in the context of a humanist project that already excludes some populations from its borders. There are many people whose pain, whose embodyminded difference, or whose access needs are never matriculated in the context of *disability:* folks who don't receive diagnoses, who don't necessarily take on disability identities, and who perhaps aren't even recognizable as disabled.

Instead, these predominantly poor and racialized populations experience "debility," the term Puar uses to identify those who are "foreclosed access to legibility and resources as disabled" (2017, xv). Elsewhere, I've problematized the simplicity with which Puar approaches the relationship between disability and debility, noting that sometimes being legible as disabled can invite further debilitation (Smilges 2022). In this case, though, I agree with Puar that *disability*'s currency within liberal humanism depends on its modulation, on the careful selection and regulation of disabled people within a system of governance. By this definition, *disability* refers not to the antithesis of abledness or to a position of totalizing abjection; instead, *disability* marks proximity to the normative subject, as defined by the latter's presumptive health, cisheteronormativity, class status, and whiteness. Proximity to normativity however near or far, remains measurable within the category of *disability*, and this measurability works to ensure a degree of subjectivity, however constricted, that distinguishes the interpellable disabled person from the massified debilitated other.

Disability's capacity to simultaneously confer and deny subjectivity is why I call it a *plasticizing ontology*. By regulating subjectivity, the category of *disability* operates in concert with white supremacy to adjudicate variations of humanness that shore up the able-normative boundaries of whiteness. Drawing on Zakiyyah Iman Jackson's *Becoming Human: Matter and Meaning in an Antiblack World,* I understand plasticity as "the fluidification of 'life' and fleshly existence" that challenges the fixed, dyadic relationships between subjects/objects and humans/nonhumans (2020, 11). While plasticity is sometimes defined as a proxy for liberal capacitation, Jackson proposes that it does more than capacitate a thing into a subject. In the context of race, plasticity also "seeks to define the essence of a black(ened) thing as infinitely mutable," such that the meaning of Blackness can be altered and repurposed again and again to suit whatever best serves white supremacy (11). The phrase "ontologized plasticity" is Jackson's way of naming the mandated incoherence of Black subjectivity within the humanist project—an incoherence that requires both racializing and bestializing processes of abjection (10). Since the end of slavery in the United States, the ontologies of black(ened) people have been simultaneously capacitated into humanity while also retaining traits of nonhuman animals. Ontologized plasticity, particularly as it is embodied by Black women, effectively (though chaotically, according to Jackson) maintains the boundary between human/nonhuman without threatening the supremacy of whiteness. Ontological plasticity forces us to think not in terms of *whether* someone's humanity is recognized but rather "what *kind* of human" they are allowed to be and in what contexts (49).

With the phrase plasticizing ontology, I am thinking alongside Jackson to consider how *disability* is operationalized in the process of ontologizing plasticity. The language is tricky here, so I want to parse things carefully. Jackson's ontological plasticity refers to a technique of racialized subjectification organized by a person's plasticity, what she describes as "an *a posteriori* virtual model of a dynamic, motile mode of antiblack arrangement" (72). In this case, plasticity generates ontology. A person becomes known by their mutability. My intention with plasticizing ontology is to name a means by which mutability can be enforced: not an ontology gleaned from plasticity but an ontology that bestows or corroborates plasticity. That is, a plasticizing ontology captures how an ontological category, such as "disabled," might initiate or sustain a person's plasticization.

As a plasticizing force, *disability* aids in the maintenance of white supremacy by, on the one hand, offering legibility to Black and otherwise racialized populations through diagnosis and disability identity while, on the other hand, ensuring the pathologization of Blackness and the reification of whiteness as the definitional ideal for health and abledness. *Disability* thus participates in competing projects of inter- and intra-human speciation. The category upholds the human/nonhuman division through its exclusivity (rendering debilitated populations fungible) and stratifies humanity itself, diagnostically quantifying degrees of normativity. This is the "burden of materiality," according to Emily Russell: "The anomalous characteristics that exclude individuals from full access to the political imaginary become the same features that structure their participation" (2011, 16). Far from being a straightforward indicator of a person's relation to power, *disability* is better understood as a spectral metric, a mile-long threshold across which humanity can be parceled and ontological plasticity extended. To be interpellated as disabled is to be ushered into or further entwined with plasticity—situated on the rolling hills of disaggregated humanity. This is a terrain that lies sandwiched between the disposable excess of the nonhuman and the impenetrable fortress of white normativity. *Disability,* in this view, is a discursive medium through which racial subjecthood can be materialized.

Importantly, I am not ignoring the ways that racial subjecthood can also materialize disability. As Dennis Tyler explains, "Any persons who pose or are perceived as a threat to the nation's collective health could be contained, injured, or even destroyed, which demonstrates how metaphors of disability are made material on Black bodies and minds" (2022, 17–18). As an embodyminded experience, disability can be a product of a person's racialization, such as through forms of targeted state violence. For others, disability can exist independently of their race, as is the case for many people with congenital disabilities. My focus here, though, is on the ontological work that the category of disability carries out as part of the humanist project. This is work that assists in securing the borders of humanity while also divvying up its splendors. *Disability* is a plasticizing ontology because it generates the requisite conditions, what Jackson calls the "bio-ontological currency," to preserve plastic life (2020, 198). The category of *disability* offers some degree of liberal recognition without necessarily posing any threat to the dominant social order. *Disability* incapacitates through its promises of capacitation, which is to say that the category of *disability* bears far more ideological weight than many people give it credit for. In much the same way that an unqualified antisocial thesis risks masking the whiteness and abledness that subtend *queer*'s conditions of emergence, so too does an overly simplistic approach to *disability*—one that misses its utility to liberal humanism—neglect to account for the category's own racial debt.

Perhaps it will seem obvious by now, but it's worth emphasizing that being disabled or claiming a disability identity says very little about a person's experience of ableism, let alone their position in the broader social hierarchy, and still less about their political orientation to their position or the hierarchy. *Disability,* it turns out, doesn't mean a whole lot by itself. Much in the same way that Marquis Bey argues that a person's racial identity is "not an a priori determinant of politicality," neither can disability be confidently or consistently tethered to an anti-ableist politic (2017, 277). As Texas governor Greg Abbott exemplifies, many disabled people do quite the opposite of anti-ableism by working within an "ideology of up-lift," to borrow from Stefano Harney and Fred Moten, which brands itself as a form of diversity work, despite ultimately functioning "in the interest of empire" (2013, 49). This iteration of anti-ableism isn't really about countering ableism—at least, not the structural force of it. Anti-ableism that is focused only on uplift, on progress, on access, on re-capacitation/cuperation/habilitation is just ableism lite. True anti-ableism requires both an awareness of power as networked and a committed pursuit of collective liberation across that network. "No body or mind can be left behind," explains the disability justice-based performance project Sins Invalid in its "10 Principles of Disability Justice," "only moving together can we accomplish the revolution we require" (2015). This is an anti-ableism with a critical wingspan broader than the category of *disability*, a politic feathered out across the variegated identities, communities, and geographies impacted by the violently uneven distribution of humanity.

When infused with crip negativity, anti-ableism further reveals that the category of *disability* is itself often both an effect and a weapon of ableism, simultaneously its product and instrument. To be sure, some people are thrust into the category of *disability* against their will, and I am certainly not suggesting such people are inher-ently ableist. Rather, I'm pointing to the tricky rhetorical machinery that drives and disguises ableism: how we've come to believe it is fueled by the selective marginalization of disabled people when it is more accurately fueled by the dispossession of all bodyminds believed to be undesirable, unproductive, and disposable. While disabled people often take on connotations of undesirability, un-productivity, and disposability, we are not their exclusive terrain. Ableism can dramatically shape the lives of people without access to the category of *disability*, and ableism routinely operates in conjunction with racism, colonialism, classism, and cisheterosexism in ways that remain illegible under the rubric of *disability*.

I am thinking of the trauma left in the wake of incarceration, of the chronic pain rendered quotidian in the sew houses operated by U.S. companies on ships in international waters, of the nutritional deficiencies among children with "lunch debt" at school, and of the depression faced by trans kids whose access to healthcare has been criminalized. Ableism hugs the contours of all these examples, despite none of them necessarily or consistently maintaining legibility as a disability. I am left to wonder, given the breadth of ableism, why the language of disability continues to be the dominant mode of engaging anti-ableism. Who benefits from organizing done within the category of *disability* if not all people bearing the brunt of ableism are disabled? Whose bodies, minds, access needs, and experiences of pain and debilitation are invisibilized in order to maintain *disability*'s categorical coherence? Is it possible that there is something rotten at the core of *disability*—not its phenomenology but its ontology?

Cripping the Future

The more I ask questions such as these, which interrogate the ideology of disability, the more overwhelmed I feel by the affective depth of crip negativity. Efforts to reclaim or politicize *disability* are no doubt well intended, but how many of them fail to reconcile with the violence of *disability*'s structuring essence? *Disability* only becomes politically tenable in a humanist context, wherein the designation "disabled" accords a person with a measure of humanness. Even if we contest the value of that designation, arguing that disability means more or differently than able-normative society would have us believe, we have not yet addressed the underlying problem, the more fundamental ableism, that allows some embodyminded conditions to be capacitated into disabilities but not others. Moreover, we neglect to account for the plasticization of *disability*'s ontology, the way it demarcates a person's distance from normativity—at once wrapping an arm around our waist and holding us at arm's length. This is *disability* as a kind of "burdened individuality," to borrow from Saidiya Hartman, that welcomes you into the room, only to leave others still outside and to leave you sitting alone by the door: your presence a symbol of equality that paints over a lingering inequity (1997, 121).

Read in this light, *disability* has no ethical future. I am willing to stake that claim, even though I will myself into believing alternative futures for *disability* are possible. Right now, I'm feeling my bad crip feelings, and all I can manage to think under the wash of negativity is that there can be no ethical future for *disability* so long as it remains defined primarily by its capacitating telos rather than its debilitated excess. Without reconciliation, there can be no collective healing. Without collective healing, there is only more wounding guised under progress. Progressive wounding is not an ethical future.

In claiming no ethical future for *disability*, I am making the equally bold claim that the core problem with Edelman's *No Future* and with the antisocial thesis more generally is not that they are too negative but that they are not negative enough. Edelman's failure to account for the dispossessed futurities of queer, trans, poor, racialized, and disabled kids was a symptom of his broader failure of imagination. It's easier to refuse the social when you can only imagine an existence in which the social has already been offered to you. It is much harder, Jack Halberstam insists, to refuse "that which was first refused to us" (2013, 12).

The antisocial thesis is limited by two, related assumptions: first, that reproductive futurism is a birthright and, second, that negativity emerges from deciding that the birthright is insufficient and choosing to relinquish it. There's no doubt that it is insufficient—reproductive and rehabilitative futurisms are not ones I have interest in pursuing—but there is a privilege laden in the capacity to indulge this kind of refusal: to be able to say "no" and yet always retain the possibility of saying "yes" at a later time. The birthright remains, no matter how often or how loudly you disavow it. For those who exist beyond the edges of society or whose entrance to society is predicated on their ontological plasticity, refusal is another game entirely. I'm talking about "the undercommons," in Harney and Moten's (2013) words, that are made up of Black and otherwise abjected people, spaces, and labor that, through their invisibilization, disavowal, or sublimation, imbue the commons with its sense of commonness. To practice refusal from the undercommons is not limited to the refusal of reproductive or rehabilitative futurisms but requires the refusal of the broader humanist project out of which such futurisms emerged in the first place. This refusal is a form of abolition, where the objective is "not so much the abolition of prisons but the abolition of a society that could have prisons" (42). It is not a refusal of the future we have mapped out for us but a refusal of the society that could believe such a future is desirable.

In the context of disability, Harney and Moten's refusal returns us to my opening discussion of access. If anti-ableism is limited to calls for greater access, it does little to challenge the conditions that produce inaccessibility. It is not enough to secure disabled people an invitation into the room, especially when such an invitation depends on the intensified obfuscation or effacement of people excluded from the category of *disability*. Access for the sake of access only maintains *disability*'s regulatory and plasticizing functions. What we need instead is a grander, more sweeping, and dare I say more negative form of anti-ableism that reveals both the immediate harm of inaccessibility as well as the legacies of ableist violence mixed into the batter of our society and its extant futurisms. This is a refusal not of a birthright but of a fantasy. It's a letting go of the dream, however soft and warm, that inaccessibility is the primary problem rather than the invitation-only room.

The purpose of crip negativity is not to usurp the work that other scholars have done to imagine new futures for disability, nor is it to dismiss the value of activist efforts to expand access in the short term. Such work and efforts are necessary corollaries to crip negativity that allow many of us to survive our refusals. Crip negativity is meant to reorient us to anti-ableism in a way that both demands more from the world and allows us the crip/trauma/mad time to feel the weight of our demands. In the short chapters that follow, each addresses what crip negativity looks like in practice, revealing it not only as an individual posture of refusal but also as a communal praxis. Even if crip negativity rejects the social as it is currently organized around able-normativity, we must still recognize the interdependence and care we all rely on to stay alive. I was surprised to discover just how much care I needed to write this little book. It takes a village for even one person to feel their bad crip feelings cripply. While writing, I depended on the shoulders, words, emojis, and kisses of so many crip and queer kin. It wasn't easy for me to follow crip negativity's affective itinerancies or to relay all that it demanded: in part because I nearly drowned plunging its depth, in part because of the hostility I knew its demands would elicit, and in part because by articulating what it wanted, I was forced to confront how much I needed.

Disabled people need more than this world has to offer. We need more than any amount of access can provide. We need more than the future can guarantee. We need more than the horizon can glimpse. We need more than a disavowal of society. We need more than a refusal of the terms we've been offered. We need so much that, as I write in the next chapter, it can be easier to silently steal what we need than to ask for it all out loud. Despite my own crip and neuroqueer commitments, I still sometimes feel embarrassed and guilty about how different my needs are from the needs of ableds around me. I know in theory that my needs are no more than anyone else's, that abled needs are simply normalized and thus invisibilized. Yet when I'm the only one at the party who needs the volume of the music turned down, when I'm the only one in the movie theater that needs to have a meltdown on the floor, when I'm the only one in the Zoom call that needs a stim break, when I'm the only one with needs that are noted and notable, it's easy to feel like asking for access, let alone asking for anything additional, is asking for simply too much.

This is one of my most common expressions of internalized ableism: feeling like I'm too much because I need too much without offering nearly enough in return. I feel like I take and take and take from everyone around me without having the capacity to give back anything of value. It's a bad crip feeling, this feeling. It's crip because I know for a fact that I'm not alone in feeling it and that, while some of the folks who feel it with me are also disabled, many are not, even as they find themselves similarly suffocated by ableism: all at once confronted by an inaccessible world, disappointed by what access has to offer, and still left feeling inadequate of the half portion of a life we're allowed to live. Crip negativity leans into the pain of this feeling, recognizing it as a necessary step toward liberation. It is only by feeling our bad crip feelings collectively, as well as cripply, that we can begin to demand all that we need to thrive. What we need is a lot, but we're worth it. We're a lot, and we're worth it.

2. Access Thievery

I'M GOING TO TELL YOU SOMETHING, but you have to swear not to tell anyone. This is just between us crips, queers, and the people who love us, okay?

I fibbed earlier today. I told a little lie. Two lies, actually. They're not something I'm proud of, but I don't regret them. At this very moment, I am supposed to be in a meeting—not a particularly important meeting but one that has been scheduled for several months and one in which my absence will be noticed. In order to get out of the meeting, I told the organizer that I wouldn't be able to attend because I had a family emergency. But I do not have a family emergency; that was a lie. In about an hour, I'm supposed to teach a class, but I canceled the class and told the students I've been vomiting. I have not, however, vomited and actually have a rather sturdy stomach. The real reason I could not attend the meeting or teach my class is because I did not want to. I did not want to attend the meeting or teach my class because I don't have the bandwidth to listen to other people today. I've peopled too much this week, and a girl is tired of stimulation.

While I generally prefer to be honest about my access needs with colleagues and students, the truth is that today is Monday, so when I say that "I've peopled too much this week," what I really mean is that I went out to dinner yesterday evening at a restaurant that was a decibel too loud, had a meltdown in the car on the way home, and am now physically/emotionally/mentally unprepared for the workweek. So the real truth is that I have a sensory hangover, which isn't something I've quite learned how to explain to non-autistic and otherwise nondisabled people who more often than not find themselves *energized* rather than depleted by excessive sensory stimulation.

What, exactly, would I tell them? "So I'm here, but just know that I will not be listening to anything you say. Also, this pained look on my face isn't necessarily about you but actually kind of is. It's not that I don't want to be here; I just don't want to be around you or see you or smell you or god forbid hear that screechy laugh you make every ten seconds." Hungover Logan is kind of a bitch. Despite the generosity and patience of my colleagues and students, it remains the case that most of them are not operating on crip/trauma/mad time. They're running to the beat of a hyperabled academic institution with all of its deadlines and schedules and chronological measures of productivity. I knew the moment I woke up this morning, though, that if I went about my Monday as scheduled, I would exacerbate my hangover, making each day this week progressively more difficult to withstand and rendering it next to impossible for me to write, to fuck my partner, to walk my dog, or to help an older friend clean her house. I told a couple of lies today because I recognized that I had access needs that would not be met if I did not meet them myself and that if I let my needs go unmet, I wouldn't be able to provide the care that I'd promised to others. As a result, I did not ask for access. I did not arrange accommodations. And I did not wait until my well-being depended on others' provision of my access. I stole the access that I needed in order to flourish. This is access thievery.

In the previous chapter, I went in pretty hard on access. Often the energy we expend demanding access from abled people and ableist institutions is wasted, whether because the access we're given isn't sufficient, the access is offered too late, or the access isn't provided at all. Other times, the availability of access isn't the problem, such as when the institutions, communities, spaces, or discourses to which we are demanding access cause harm to others. There are lots of reasons for us to be suspicious of any disability politic that is focused more on securing disabled people's entrance into a broken system than interrogating the brokenness of the system itself. Yet, there are still times when access is necessary.

For me, necessary access is constituted not only by the access we need to survive (e.g., food, shelter, healthcare, etc.) but also the access we need to thrive. I don't think it's particularly outrageous to believe that survival, alone, is not a desirable threshold for a life worth living. Everyone, including disabled people, deserve to thrive. We deserve to flourish. We deserve joy and pleasure and deep laughter. These things are not privileges, rewards we should have to earn through labor, or scarce resources we should have to ration. Sufficient access should include access to the lives we want for ourselves. This is the kind of access I mean when I talk about access thievery. It's not only that we are stealing access but also that we are redefining what access means in the process. We're not settling for survival. We're stealing for our flourishing. We're stealing because we're owed the opportunity to thrive; we're allowed to demand more for ourselves than just barely enough.

Criminal Crips

Before we go any further, let's check in with each other. How are you doing? How are you feeling? If you're anything like me, it might be a bit uncomfortable to talk about access in terms of theft. Regardless of our needs, it can be difficult to ask for help, let alone to take it without asking. Many of us have been accused of lying, of laziness, of selfishness, or of moral ineptitude because of our access needs. I cannot tell you how many times I've been told by relatives, friends, colleagues, and boyfriends that they cannot trust me—not because I've fibbed about needing to miss meetings but because they perceive my emotions as insincere or fake. Unless I exert tremendous energy to mask my autism by performing neurotypicality, I am routinely perceived as a fraudulent human, as a shifty, suspicious figure whose tears come too easily, whose laughter bursts too suddenly, whose eyes fade to a hollow stare. For years, I did everything I could to earn back people's trust that I'd never had in the first place, even if it meant ignoring my own access needs. I felt it my responsibility to compensate for others' ableism. But there came a point when I realized that it's not worth the energy to justify the access I need to flourish. It's not my job to explain ableism to itself. If a person or institution is already loaded with prejudice against disabled people, presuming our immorality, fine—whatever. But I'm going to take my access regardless because I need it. Because my needs are more important to me than their opinion of me. Because what I need in order to flourish today carries more weight than their ableism steeped in yesterday.

The truth of the matter is that abled people have been fantasizing about the dangers of evil crips for centuries. These fantasies emerge from a moral model of disability that is drenched in rhetorics of racism, cisheterosexism, and classism that all assign moral value to embodied difference. Even before the category of *disability* existed in its present form, there were variations of ableism rooted in the belief that some "monstrous" bodyminds were predisposed to vice (Bearden 2019). These antiquated fears of monstrosity underpin contemporary assumptions about the untrustworthiness of disabled people. These assumptions are not so much consciously held as they are embedded into the fabric of our society, shaping everything from welfare programs to truancy laws to the definition of citizenship.

Since the founding of the United States, variations of the moral model of disability have been called upon to constrict and surveil the civic role of marginalized populations. Disabled, racialized, trans, queer, and poor people have been routinely excluded from the democratic process because of their alleged predisposition to criminality, and these populations' collective absence has helped to secure the entitlements of the white, cisheteroabled upper class (Dolmage 2018). Using formal legislation to fuse disability and deviance, the United States has been able to maintain ideals of physical fitness and mental acuity as metrics for the moral purity of white supremacy and, by extension, national identity. So long as disability and disabled people are regarded with suspicion—our experiences debated, our intentions questioned, our efforts doubted—the desirability and ontological coherence of abledness remain uninterrogated. Then, by suturing abledness to whiteness, disability is effectively racialized, further entrenching the criminalization of racial difference, especially Blackness. The grounds on which disabled people are politically disenfranchised depend not only on allegorizing disability to criminality but also purporting it as evidence of racial degeneration.

In his stunning analysis of "civic disabilities" in the nineteenth century, Andrew Dilts (2012) reveals that denying suffrage to disabled and incarcerated people has long been a legislative strategy used to restrict the rights of African Americans. Disability's proximity to criminality was legally codified in a number of states during the years leading up to the Civil War because of the perceived threat that freed Black people posed to the white polity. "As developmentally arrested, and therefore naturally non-autonomous," Dilts explains, "persons marked as criminal, idiotic, or black were assumed to be unable to *work* or even *think* independently, and therefore could not take part in the practice of self-government." By explicitly disenfranchising incarcerated and disabled people, legislators were able to simultaneously protect the integrity of the white vote while "disarm[ing] claims of racial animus." Since neither incarcerated people nor disabled people are *exclusively* Black populations, the racial logics underpinning their disenfranchisement are not always obvious.

Nevertheless, reflecting on the collective marginalization of incarcerated, disabled, and Black people today, Dilts points out that "U.S. jails and prisons have once again become Jim Crow asylums, filled primarily with persons of color, a shockingly high number of whom are mentally ill, and nearly all of whom are stripped of the vote." The stereotype of the monstrously evil crip has evolved into the criminal crip: both are decipherable within a racial matrix that harnesses abledness as a vector of whiteness. Presumed competence and righteousness subtend the white abled person in such a way that adheres disability and criminality through color-blind racism (for more on the ableism of color-blind racism, see Tyler 2022). In line with a crip negative approach to the category of *disability,* the figures of the evil crip and criminal crip not only haunt legibly disabled people but also threaten anyone who falls outside the racialized boundaries of embodyminded normativity.

Among the primary reasons I am attracted to the metaphor of access thievery is that theft—as both an economic practice and criminalized activity—gestures toward a genealogy for disability activism that is attuned to the racial grammar structuring the relationship between disability and criminality. Access thievery pulls the triangulation of race, disability, and criminality into focus by repurposing it as a practice of collective freedom, a means to pursue flourishing for multiple communities with a range of relationships to institutional access. For many folks, the only access available is stolen or foraged. Requesting access or accommodations from schools, employers, or government agencies is more difficult for those who are unhoused, unemployed, incarcerated, or undocumented. Institutional access itself becomes inaccessible when a person or population is excluded from an institution, even and perhaps especially when a person's experience of exclusion causes or exacerbates their access needs. Access thievery becomes a way to name an alternative economy of access in which the needs generated by exclusionary institutions or institutional neglect are met in ways outside, beyond, or in addition to the access provided by those institutions. That is to say, access thievery is one kind of theft begotten by another: the crime of stealing access produced by the crime of systemic marginalization. Access thievery, like all forms of resistance, is simultaneously energizing for its liberatory impulse and harrowing for its conditions of emergence.

As I'm writing, I am thinking of Laurence Ralph's (2012) discussion of "trade in injury" among Chicago's gang members. For some Black and brown youth, gang membership promises forms of kinship and economic stability that are not always available in urban communities that have been gutted by police violence and gentrifi-cation. Among Chicago's gangs, disability is sometimes weaponized as a revenge tactic—disablement traded back and forth across rival groups. Ralph argues that injury, as threat and frequent obligation, structures relations between gang members, across gangs, and with-in communities wherein gang violence is common. On one hand, this injury acts as a form of "wounding," bringing to mind both the experience of disablement and the conditions that produce it, including "the drug trade, or the criminalization of black urbani-ties." On the other hand, injury also acts as a form of "enabling" by mobilizing community efforts to reduce the frequency and effects of gang violence for future generations. This organizing is itself a kind of access thievery—one that culls together mentorship and educational opportunities for youth from the vestiges of violence and debilitation.

As an example, Ralph describes a community-run program called "In My Shoes," wherein disabled ex-gang members lecture high school students on the effects of gang violence. The speakers recall their own experiences in gangs and the effects that violence has had on their lives. When talking about their injuries, the speakers "build their narratives out of the medical model of disability, in order to emphasize the biological reality of their now 'broken' body." These narratives operate as crip negative testimonies to highlight "the scale of the social problems that African Americans growing up in violent neighborhoods face." Rather than adopt a social or political model of disability that would pull focus away from their individual bodies and toward larger structures of power, these speakers lean into the "the sympathy, disgust, fear, and perhaps even the relief at being able-bodied" that the audience feels toward the spectacle of their disabilities. This approach, however distinct from typical disability advocacy, helps to draw attention to both the personal and community effects of gang violence.

When injury is traded within an extralegal economy, there is often little that can be done for the injured party, except forgive the injurer or exact revenge on the injured's behalf. Rarely can injured gang members appeal to authorities or institutions for help meeting their access needs; instead, they are left "to care for themselves," to find and assemble their own access. By sharing intimate details about their self-care routines with high school students, the "In My Shoes" speakers effectively rehearse the context in which access thievery occurs while also foraging an alternative, predictive access for the audience. As Ralph puts it, the speakers "essentially disempower themselves in order to empower others." The access that the "In My Shoes" speakers generate is intended to preemptively address the threat of injury facing students. This is a form of access operating within a crip negative temporality, wherein the concern about future injury is motivated by bad feelings surrounding gang violence in the present. Access to a less violent future is stolen and reappropriated from the compounded effects of institutional neglect, criminalization, and racialized debilitation. This is a mode of anti-ableism fueled by anti-violence at multiple scales.

It is worth suggesting that the true power and potential of access thievery lies less in its capacity to secure access to the world we already inhabit than the world we want for ourselves and our communities. We're not only stealing access that others refuse to give us but also channeling that access to critique or undercut the people and systems who have refused us access. Access thievery puts pressure on the temporal and phenomenological boundaries of disability, exposing how access might refer not only to meeting disabled people's present needs but also to heralding community wisdom to reduce the risk of injury, to prevent violence, and to manage expectations of debilitation.

Access thievery brings into stark relief what Jean Franzino (2016) describes as "disability in shades of grey" or when "the line between 'disability' and 'ability'" is uncertain. It may seem counterintuitive to align anti-ableism with efforts to lessen the frequency of disability, given the long history of eugenic initiatives intended to eradicate disabled people. But it is important to keep in mind the multiple and entangled vectors of power at work in the process of becoming disabled, especially among racialized, queer and trans, and poor communities. It is only by thinking across differences in the experience of disability that anti-ableism can be a vector of collective liberation. Sometimes this means centering forms of and relations to disability that do not circulate frequently in the field of disability studies, such as those occasioned by violence, by trauma, or by neglect and, as such, can be regarded as loss or as tragedy. Thinking with these forms of disability opens up conversations about whose needs are considered access needs, thereby urging a democratization of the field of disability studies that is more expansively attuned to the range of individuals who are fighting against ableism, including those who remain skeptical of disability's desirability. Taking a cue from Alison Kafer (2017), access thievery might be best understood as a crip negative practice of "rebel health," which "attends to health's others, refusing to see health as a weapon or as a zero-sum game." Rather than remain fixated on providing institutional access to people we already designate as disabled, access thievery blossoms outward toward those folks for whom institutional access is *or would be* difficult to secure. Access thievery is stealing what we need because we need it. It is foraging what we know you need because we once needed it. It is sharing what we have because that's what we do. It is building a "we" where there was none before because it is only wrapped in each other's arms that we can do more than survive.

Sexual Access

To end this chapter, I'd like to share the example of access thievery that first started me thinking about the concept and one that remains close to my heart. Some of you may be familiar with the Netflix show *Special*, a semi-autobiographical comedy starring Ryan O'Connell, a gay, white man with cerebral palsy. One of the first season's central plot lines follows Ryan as he tries to lose his virginity. Like many disabled people, Ryan finds it difficult to navigate sexual relationships, especially in the gay community where whiteness, abledness, and thinness are the bastions of desirability.

At the suggestion of a friend, Ryan chooses to hire a sex worker to be his first sexual partner. Played by Brian Jordan Alvarez, the sex worker Shea expertly guides Ryan through his first time. The audience sees Ryan's initial nervousness fade away as Shea does what he was hired to do, offering Ryan access to sexual knowledge and pleasure that he was struggling to find elsewhere. While interviews with O'Connell reveal a rather sanitized, liberal motivation behind the scene, I'd like to suggest an alternative reading that proposes erotic labor as a site for access thievery, an opportunity for critical solidarity between anti-ableist and anti-capitalist movements.

Following the premiere of *Special* in 2019, LGBTQ media outlets were excited to celebrate the casting of a gay, disabled actor to play a gay, disabled character. Couched in familiar commentary on the importance of representation, almost every article about the show mentions the sex scene described above. When asked to explain his intention with the scene, O'Connell frequently refers to his own, positive experiences with sex workers and his desire to destigmatize erotic labor. "I think there's still a level of shame with using a sex worker and this idea of feeling like you have to pay for it," he told *Pride*. "I think that ya know, do what you gotta do and don't feel any shame in doing it. It is what it is" (Henderson 2019). In other interviews, O'Connell refers to his hopes to "humaniz[e] sex work" (Kirst 2019) and to "acknowledge" disabled people's sexuality (Ryan 2019). The value of the scene, for him, lies in its capacity to normalize erotic labor by demonstrating the expertise of sex workers and their value for some disabled people who find paying for sex more accessible than other modes of sexual engagement. As admirable as O'Connell's intentions for the scene may be, I don't think they do justice to the political potentialities that it ultimately gestures toward. I am certainly not opposed to destigmatizing erotic labor or visibilizing disabled people's sexualities, but both these goals are rather tame, given the intensified levels of policing that both disabled people and sex workers face.

What I find exciting about a sex scene between a gay, disabled person and a sex worker is not its potential to normalize but its potential to align twinned queernesses: that of gay sex with a disabled person and that of erotic labor. Both are aberrant practices within the context of a society that idealizes monogamous, hetero-abled love as the most esteemed form of intimacy. More importantly, their appearance together highlights the solidarity that access thievery can generate. In the scene, Ryan isn't stealing sexual access from Shea; he's purchasing it through an extralegal, crip economy that runs counter to the forms of capitalism that structure heteronormativity. What's being stolen is not the sex itself but access to sex, which Shea offers as a paid labor. Despite institutional and cultural prohibitions against disabled people having sex (Siebers 2012; Gill 2015), Ryan smuggles it for himself with Shea's assistance.

Likewise, we can imagine Shea's erotic labor as itself a form of access thievery that forages economic survival while refusing conventional waged work. femi babylon has argued that there is something deeply liberating about channeling erotic labor into an anti-work agenda. Attempting to normalize erotic labor by calling it "work" is, for her, a kind of "half-assed reform" (babylon and Berg 2021, 633). Proposing erotic labor as an example of access thievery is to lean into its anti-capitalist potential, what Vanessa Carlisle has described as "a politics of self-worth and community care" (2021, 577). In Shea's case, the theft occurring is not interpersonal—he is not stealing from Ryan, nor is Ryan stealing from him—but structural. Shea is stealing a livelihood from an economy in which the forms of labor that constitute legally sanctioned work are narrowly defined and heavily surveilled. Together, Shea and Ryan are building a counter-economy through access thievery, one in which mutual care acts as a currency for collective survival.

In the show, we are not told very much about Shea. He only appears in one scene as a light-skinned, muscular man. There is no reason to assume that he, like Ryan, is disabled; he might not even actually be gay. However, it's worth acknowledging that many sex workers are disabled or otherwise marginalized and choose to pursue erotic labor because it offers varying degrees of access that are unavailable through conventional employment (babylon 2019). Zia

Moon, a sex worker with a chronic illness, has written at length about how well-suited erotic labor is to her own and other disabled people's needs. "Certain sick folks must navigate a gray area," she explains. "What do you do if you're too sick to hold down a full-time job, yet not 'sick enough' for disability benefits, and a typical part-time job isn't enough to survive on—especially with medical bills?" (2018). Hayley Jade, a neurodivergent sex worker, agrees: erotic labor is "the perfect job for someone with ADHD and autism because there's a routine but there's also variety in my clients and how we spend our time" (2021a). Jade adds elsewhere that she appreciates being able to work with disabled clients, noting that "we're both contributing so much to each other's lives" (2021b). In her case, erotic labor is a rare opportunity to steal access for herself and remain in community with other disabled people by offering a service that many of us need. Access thievery is how she takes and how she gives.

Jade's experience resonates with the scene from *Special* insofar as they both capture access thievery's bilateral movement. Between sex workers and their disabled clients, access thievery works in two directions: applying to the clients who secure intimacy outside the strictures of institutionalized heteronormative monogamy and to the workers who push back against their exploitation under capitalism. Both figures steal access for themselves and for each other. Their thefts accumulate or interanimate as mutual resistance to sexual ableism and ableist capitalism. What Ryan steals is simultaneously invested into Shea's flourishing; what Shea forages is redistributed as Ryan's access. This is stealing the access we need to thrive ourselves so that we might be better equipped to aid and abet others' criminalized modes of indulging joy and manifesting pleasure. Theft that enables more theft. Access doubling up on itself—multiplying. It's pilfering a little time, a little energy, a little money, or a little affection in order to reinvest these same resources into others who need them.

Access thievery is all of the ways I do bad things in order to honor my whole person. Sometimes I need to be reminded that I am a whole person worth honoring. Sometimes I need help replenishing my spirit, so I can honor your whole person because you, too, are a whole person worth honoring. While I wish we didn't have to steal our flourishing, having to steal it doesn't make it any less ours. It might not seem particularly honorable to fabricate excuses for missing meetings now and then, but I'm unsure that honor was ever in the cards for me. And that's fine. I don't need honor; I just need to go back to bed.

3. Life Strike

YOU SHOULD KNOW before reading this chapter that I have put off writing it as long as possible. While I do not typically procrastinate, this chapter has been an exception because I feel guilty writing it. I feel guilty because what I'm writing is as much a lesson I need to learn as it is an argument I believe others need to read.

This chapter is largely about the labor of crip life, the work of living with disability, and I will be the first to admit that I am not proud of my relationships with labor or work. It's not only that I work too much but also that I struggle to know myself outside of my labor. It's embarrassing, honestly, how little I know about myself beyond the labor I do. When I strip away the pages I've read this week, the words I've typed since breakfast, the lessons I've planned so far this semester, the conferences I've attended, the committees I've sat on, the faculty meetings I've endured, the office hours I've held—what's left?

Part of me wants to insist that quite a lot is left. I have a vigorous exercise routine. I have a partner I love, and we have a home and dog we care for. I have friends. I have recipes I enjoy following and television shows I watch. I have a meticulous skin care routine. I have a farmer's market I visit on Saturdays. I have a life, flourishing and full. But another part of me, the more candid part that my crip negativity is drudging up—kicking and screaming from the pit of my stomach—is less certain about the quality of my life outside of my labor. This candid part of me feels compelled to admit that the majority of my exercise is dedicated to detoxifying my body from the stress of my job. My partner has threatened to leave me numerous times because he says I spend too much time at the office. I rarely see my friends, and I can barely keep up with their texts. I haven't made any of my favorite recipes in months because I've been too tired, and I often fall asleep midway through trying to watch an episode of anything. My skin is breaking out constantly, regardless of what I lather on top of it. The farmer's market is actually a Costco. I have a life, but it is sad and hanging on by a thread. I'm sad and hanging on by a thread. I'm working too much, but I don't know how to stop. Not really, truly stop. I'm not even sure I know what stopping would look like. This chapter is meant to be a move in the right direction—a move toward saying "enough is enough," a move toward tapping out until the conditions change, a move toward striking on life as I know it.

In the previous chapter, I proposed access thievery as a daily praxis, a way of orienting ourselves toward others and mobbing through the world together to ensure our collective access needs are met. Access thievery is about scavenging ways to make life work when there's no other option. Sometimes we have to do less-than-respectable things in order to make do with the conditions of our life as it is. This chapter, though, leans more deeply into the grim absolution of crip negativity. Here I want to consider what happens when life *isn't working* or *can't work any longer*. By "life," I am referring to the assemblage of activities that occupy our time. For many of us, the majority of life's activities are in some way re-lated to labor, whether paid labor (e.g., working a job and keeping up a side hustle) or unpaid labor (e.g., caregiving and domestic re-sponsibilities). There is also the labor of life itself: our bodyminds require labor to sustain themselves over time. Feeding them, bath-ing them, keeping them warm and dry, offering them rest, exercis-ing them, caring for them when they are injured or in pain are all forms of life's labor. Much like the heart organ must labor continuously to pump the body with fresh blood, so too must each of us labor on our bodies in order to keep ourselves alive.

For crips, the labor of our living takes on additional, rhetorical heft because of the stigma surrounding our "special needs." Despite the fact that all people, disabled and nondisabled alike, require labor to live, disabled people shoulder an especial burden for the labor that goes into our maintenance, and we are made aware of our own burdensomeness every day. From the sympathetic looks we watch our parents receive while we're growing up, to the human resource manager begrudgingly offering us our accommodations, to the televised politicians blaming the national debt on our measly welfare checks, we are well aware of how others perceive the labor that keeps us alive. It is perceived as too much labor, unnecessary labor, labor with a poor rate of return, wasted labor.

We are aware, also, of how much unrecognized labor we take on as a result of these perceptions: the endless paperwork to secure benefits, unending calls to the insurance company, frequent trips to the disability services office, requests to move pharmacies, upping the number of appointments with our therapists, and stints in the hospital or rehab occasioned by the intensified stress on our bodyminds. Plus, there are all of the minor inconveniences—the time-sucks—that accompany being disabled in a world built for ableds, such as waiting on an accessible parking spot to open up, having to roll around to the back of the building to find a ramp, charging the batteries for a hearing aid or prosthetic, delaying a meeting until the interpreter arrives, asking people to repeat themselves multiple times because they're speaking too quickly or with an affective intensity that doesn't register, needing to clean the desk a second time before lunch because your coworker used it without asking, or demanding virtual options for an event (yet again) because there's a goddamn pandemic. The great irony of people blaming disabled folks for requiring too much labor is that those people don't know half of the labor we actually require or that much of it is a direct result of the obstacles they put in front of us. There is so much crip labor wrapped up in being disabled, and much of it is just navigating different shades of ableism.

When I say that I want to consider in this chapter what happens when life isn't working, part of what I'm referring to is the overwhelming amount of uniquely crip labor that disabled people find themselves performing. It's so much; it's too much. But the clause "life isn't working" refers also to how the labor of life can infringe on parts of our lives that are not meant to be work, that were not originally labor but have come to adopt its qualities. This infringement often takes shape as exhaustion, overstimulation, or irritability that makes it difficult for us to give time and attention to the things we care about without feeling like we are laboring even more. The laboriousness of life turning life itself into labor until we can't even distinguish between the two. It's a degree of overwork that plasters work over everything we do.

It's as if we have clocked into a job called living and don't know how to go on break or head home for the night. Everything feels like a chore. Every conversation becomes an item on a to-do list. Every text, an obligation. Every walk or roll outside, an insult to an already tired body. Every meal, an annoying interruption of the day's agenda. On and on. It becomes increasingly difficult to differentiate between labor and nonlabor when everything makes you feel the same way: tired, sad, indifferent, empty, lonely, bored, frustrated, anxious, angry, overwhelmed, or any of the crip negative feelings that limn the experience of disability. The flavor of labor intensifies until you can't taste anything else. The labor required to sustain your life dissolves into a pool of labor-living that makes it nearly impossible to recognize life outside your labor. This is when you know your life can't work any longer as it is. Life isn't working when life itself feels like work.

A *life strike* is a crip negative response to the work of life or to chronic labor-living. Inspired by anti-work politics and labor movement rhetoric, a life strike pursues a total relinquishing of all labor beyond what is required for our sustenance. Life striking may include refusing waged work, but such a refusal is neither required nor sufficient. Life striking is a broader bowing out, a spiritual re-trenchment, a pulling back into oneself as a way to call oneself forth again. To strike from life is to strike from the modes of relation and integration organized around labor that claim to know us, to define us, and to make us whole. To strike from life is to die to the world as it's extracted and sold back to us, so we might find in ourselves another life—another way to live—that is more attuned to the body-minds we have, to how we want to occupy them, and to how we want them to occupy the world.

Cripping Labor Politics

Bringing questions about disability and labor together, as a life strike does, is a well-established practice in the disability community. Labor politics have been at the center of disability activism in the United States since the latter's inception. As I describe in the first chapter, much of the impetus behind the disability rights movement in the 1970s was to advance educational and career opportunities for disabled people, thereby providing more accessible pathways to enter the workforce. As Tanya Aho argues, however, disability's labor politics have historically done less to radicalize either labor or the category of *disability* than it has to produce variations of "labor-normativity" that domesticate the disabled citizen through waged work. Labor-normativity instrumentalizes the language of access and accessibility to secure disabled people's employment "as a driving force of one's life, a significant site of identity construc-tion, and the major influence on one's life cycle, daily rhythm, and imagined future" (2017, 322). By consistently centering issues of labor access and workplace accessibility without attending to the violence of labor-normativity, much of disability rights activism has embraced labor-living as necessary to our liberal citizenship and to our legibility as subjects.

Despite the importance of securing equitable opportunities and protections for disabled workers, we cannot forget that neither op-portunities nor protections within neoliberal capitalism address the fundamental problem of liberal humanism—the true target of crip negativity's bad feelings. Regardless of the efforts we make toward more and better jobs for disabled people, it remains the case that labor-normativity is designed to produce labor-living; that is, to induct disabled people into a socioeconomic system that disguises labor as life. This disguise works effectively so long as some forms of difference can be recuperated as marketable commodities while others continue to mark fungible populations for targeted debilitation. In the context of disability, access to labor cannot be achieved under capitalism without crystalizing the boundaries around the category of *disability*. Such crystallization ultimately obfuscates people's crip labor, which does not aid the means of production, and further ossifies the disposability of people living on or beyond the margins of *disability*. In other words, it becomes more difficult to adduce the debilitating, stratified violence of labor-living when laboring itself is cited as evidence only of a person's successful rehabilitation into social and civic life. How can we recognize when life isn't working, for ourselves or others, if work is meant to make life worth living?

Unfortunately, answering this question becomes all the more challenging when we begin to unpack the layers of labor-normativity that have come to structure the scope and terms of contemporary disability politics. Some layers are relatively easy to parse, such as those commercialized variations of disability activism that trade in representation and visibility. A recent Victoria's Secret ad campaign featuring multiple disabled models comes to mind (Miranda 2022). Efforts such as these are typically engineered to demonstrate a company's or institution's inclusivity by displaying disabled workers (e.g., lingerie models) or by acknowledging disabled people as a contingent of consumers (e.g., lingerie buyers). Bestowed with the capacity to both produce and consume, labor-normativity suggests, disabled people can effectively fold themselves into the social citizenship of neoliberal capitalism.

Other layers of labor-normativity can be trickier to identify. Consider, for instance, the forms of disability advocacy that aim to broaden the horizon of employment opportunities for disabled people (Owen and Harris 2012). Since many welfare programs, excluding the dramatically underfunded Supplemental Security Income (SSI), require a current or recent employment record, disabled people are often forced to compete for unsafe and underpaid jobs. Even with antidiscrimination laws in place, many disabled people struggle to find work, especially work that is relevant to their passions and interests. As a result, those who do secure employment wind up hesitant to raise concerns about the conditions of their labor for fear of retaliation (Kumar, Sonpal, and Hiranandani 2012). Expanding employment opportunities promises to alleviate the pressure placed onto disabled workers to settle for undesirable jobs, and it shifts the burden of competition to employers, encouraging them to improve working conditions to attract and retain employees. Within this framework, the law of supply and demand is reappropriated to demonstrate a demand for work among disabled people with the hopes of stimulating a rise in the supply of accessible and desirable jobs.

The problem with reappropriating the law of supply and demand is that it acquiesces to capitalism as a necessary condition for achieving equity for disabled people. As Nirmala Erevelles argues, creating more jobs neglects to address the fact that access to waged work is an individual solution to a systemic problem. Increasing employment opportunities may extend social citizenship to some disabled people, but it also reinforces the contingence of social citizenship on employment—a contingence that capitalism weaponizes against the most vulnerable populations. Under capitalism, there will never be enough work to go around; labor must remain competitive. Those individuals deemed least likely to aid in "the accumulation of profit," which generally include people with intellectual disabilities, folks with limited access to education, people with a history of incarceration, and undocumented people, will never be offered safe and reliable employment—at least, not until another fungible population comes to take their place (2002, 19). People occupying this category of state-sponsored precarity become "immaterial citizens" whose primary function is to bear the brunt of capitalism's failures (21). Since it is an essential condition of capitalism that demand outpace supply, an entire class of individuals must remain out of work in order for the total supply of jobs to remain lower than the demand for them. The resulting, requisite class of nonworkers is not only blamed for failing to fulfill their civic-qua-consumer responsibilities under neoliberalism but also strategically excluded from social citizenship in order to preserve the currency of citizenship itself.

Efforts to improve employment opportunities for disabled people are steeped in the rhetoric of integrative access that fuels labor-normativity. Entrance to the workforce only appears liberatory in a context in which labor remains a metric for human valuation. It seems to me that the most productive—by which I mean politically generative—relationship between disability and labor is one that refuses to be such a metric. Rather than wedging the category of *disability* into neoliberalism as a meager modification to capitalism, it is worth asking whether *disability* might launch a more fundamental challenge to labor-normativity. What if there were a crip labor politics that cared less about disabled people's employment or employability than about cripping labor and interrogating the ableist conditions under which labor-living is rendered quotidian?

This question has already been answered in part by disability justice activists who have imagined models of care, mutual aid, and interdependence that sidestep the compulsory nature of work under capitalism to embrace community networks that celebrate each person's unique strengths and capacities. I am especially fond of Leah Lakshmi Piepzna-Samarasinha's thinking on "care webs" that proposes care as a "collective responsibility," a social mapping of what people need and what they can offer (2018, 33). The metaphor of a web gestures toward care's scope and complexity. Care should not be reducible to static roles of giver and receiver, nor should only one person be responsible for all of the care that another person needs. Instead, care should be distributed across a community. We each maintain different skillsets, privileges, and levels of access to resources that others need at different times, in different ways, and to different degrees. The care that my lover offers me is different from the care I offer him; likewise, the care I offer my lover is not the same that I offer my friend Gavin—nor is the care he gives me the same that I pay my therapist to provide. Care takes as many shapes as the bodyminds that require it. Similar to bodyminds, care is fluid, situated, personalized, and sometimes intimate. Care can also be exhausting, frustrating, laced with jealousy or resentment, and at times overwhelming.

Another reason I admire Piepzna-Samarasinha on the topic of care is their willingness to wrestle with the challenges that accompany sustaining care webs in a society that remains unsuited to such community-based forms. Caregiving burnout can happen. Access friction is real. What I need and what others have to offer do not always align. What I have to give isn't always what others demand. Sometimes two people's needs rub up against each other in a way that hurts our hearts. "I've often seen crip-only spaces fill with feelings of betrayal and hopelessness when we cannot fulfill some of our friends' needs," Piepzna-Samarasinha admits (65). It's easy to feel let down by our communities when our care needs go unmet. It's even easier to feel angry when others ask us for care while we're still waiting to receive care ourselves. The challenge of care webs is not building them but maintaining them through the rain, dust, and wind that are grief, difference, and change. This maintenance is its own kind of crip labor that, while necessary in the long battle against neoliberal capitalism, comes at a steep cost. The cost is labor-living: feeling like the care we are meant to gladly give is yet another form of work. Extractive. Depletive. Debilitative. Sometimes even our efforts to liberate ourselves from work can feel like more of the same. Sometimes the work of cripping labor ends up crippling us.

How to Strike a Life

It is in recognition of life's many, overlapping labors—waged and unwaged, economic and relational, social and personal—that I am convinced of the need for a life strike. As an intentional and temporary lapse of labor, a life strike erects boundaries around oneself in order to heal from the wounds of labor-living. Admittedly, a life strike is unsustainable and, not unlike efforts to create more jobs, an individualistic response to a systemic problem. However, unlike the individualism of waged work, which is meant to conceal the structural flaws of capitalism, the individualism of a life strike empowers each of us to honor our unique needs to ensure the long-term sustainability of care-based communities. It is a way for me to acknowledge when the life I'm living has become too laborious, perhaps so much so that it doesn't feel much like a life at all anymore.

A life strike could take many forms, depending on the severity of a person's labor wounds and the material conditions of their lives. In an ideal world, people could strike from life quite literally and hibernate like bears for months at a time. I wish people could quit their jobs and delete their email accounts and hole up in a cabin in the woods or spread out on a beach or hike an entire continent with no timeline or schedule. For some folks, these kinds of strikes are possible, and for those folks, I am genuinely so happy. But the reality is that most of us cannot afford to strike from life in such a way because we have laborious responsibilities that cannot be feasibly or ethically avoided. I'm thinking of parents with young children. I'm thinking of disabled adults who require assistance with one or more daily tasks. I'm thinking of people with limited incomes or who have frequent doctors' appointments or who are incarcerated or who are the primary caregivers for a partner, family member, or friend. I'm thinking of most of us, for whom the possibility of a consummate life strike just isn't going to happen.

I would like to believe, nevertheless, that life striking does not need to be totalizing in order to be valuable. As Kathi Weeks explains in her crucial book *The Problem with Work,* a refusal of work according to an anti-work politics "is not a renunciation of labor *tout court,* but rather a refusal of the ideology of work" (2011, 99). Life striking is not only about ending the practice of labor-living but also about revising our orientation to labor-normativity. Crip negativity exposes labor-normativity for what it is: a prime example of the fundamental failures of liberal humanism expressed through neoliberal capitalism. Crip negativity invites our bad feelings toward the ideology of work. It also recognizes our collective existence in relation to this ideology, as well as the ways this ideology shapes and delimits the feasible refusals at our disposal. Crip negativity allows us to reject the world as it is and yet remain cognizant of our place in it. Life striking, as a practice of crip negativity, is no exception: it is at once ambitious in its intention and flexible in its terms. A life strike might mean quitting a job, but it might also mean cutting back your hours. A life strike could include a lengthy getaway to a remote location, but it could also be a long weekend in your apartment with no scheduled events. A life strike might be cutting ties with someone, but it might also be a series of honest conversations that clarify your boundaries. Borrowing from Sunaura Taylor, a life strike "implies a right not to work as well as a right to live," which is to say that the purpose of striking isn't only to refuse labor but also to allow our festering bad crip feelings to break open a new life (2004, 11). A new life unbound or undefined by the labor we perform. A new life that is irreducible to our labor, whether that labor is work or care or self-sustenance. A new life that "challenges the mode of life now defined by and subordinated to work" (Weeks 99). A new life that is filled with living.

As I admit earlier in this chapter, I make no claim to knowing what a living-filled life is like. I am still in pursuit of it, still in the process of renegotiating my relationship with labor. I'm still figuring out how to strike from my own life. At the moment, I am learning how to rest, utterly and deeply. I am taking comfort in the guidance of Tricia Hersey's Nap Ministry, which explains, despite its name, that rest is "about more than naps" (2020b). Rest, which is one form that a life strike might take, is inventive. Situated at the nexus of Black liberation theology, womanism, Afrofuturism, reparations theory, somatics, and community organizing, the Nap Ministry theorizes rest as "layered, nuanced and an experimentation" that lends itself to improving the conditions of our world by giving us the time and space to imagine it differently (Hersey 2021). By envisioning my life strike as a restful experimentation, I can admit that I don't know what its results will be or how it will end for me. Bowing out from labor-living doesn't always require a plan for ducking back in. Sometimes deciding to strike is enough for now; deciding to rest is enough for now; choosing to experiment with your "enough!" can be enough for now. And then in time . . .

Perhaps my strike will encourage someone else to strike as well—in their own way and suited to their own labor-living injuries. Life striking, like all crip negative practices, is most powerful when it encourages our bad crip feelings to be felt collectively. While there is value laden in each of our individual strikes, a single strike does not harness the communal energy that crip negativity promises. It is only "when we stand in the gaps for each other and decide to be relentless in our support and witness," Hersey writes of rest, that "we can shift community" (2020a). Standing in the gaps means listening when someone says they're too tired or trusting that others will listen when you admit you're exhausted. It means taking over when someone says they can't make it or being gentle with yourself when you're the one who doesn't come. It means showing up when someone says they need you and being brave enough to ask for help when you need it. It means expecting that sometimes everyone in your care web will need life strikes at once and being willing to stick it out through conversations after midnight to ensure everyone gets what they need.

Life striking, though demanded individually, is practiced in community. It is with "a radical understanding of interconnectedness," says Hersey (2020a), that we can collectively negotiate refusal. Both one at a time and all together, we insist that we are not doing this anymore. We will not take part. We will not give more of ourselves. We refuse the access we've been given. It is not enough; it is too late; it is to a room we don't want to occupy. We are taking a nap. We are breaking up. We are leaving. We are done for now, for today, for forever. We are indulging our bad crip feelings. We are on strike.

4. Cripping Critique

DURING MY senior year of high school, I wrote a book of poems. It was never published, but I did print out the manuscript and place it next to the cake at my graduation party. Typical of high school poetry, the book is very sad and not very good. There is a lot of rhyming for no particular reason. My experiments with abstraction constantly lose track of themselves. There are metaphors that I barely understood at the time, followed up by recollections of experiences I'd never actually had. The whole thing was written as though I were the first person to have ever felt anything. The book took on the martyred tone of a boy who had yet to learn how to situate his pain.

In retrospect, the thought of sharing the book with others makes me cringe. No one needs to read the performed intellectualism of my teenage self. But the book is nevertheless an important artifact in my personal archive because it documents some of my first attempts to articulate my bad crip feelings. I cherish the manuscript for its affective purity. Recalling my nickname at the time, Awkward John, I know that I wrote the book with all of the anger and sadness and embarrassment and longing and despair that I'd accumulated over the years living beneath that name. Awkward John produced the feelings that produced the book. Awkward John as description and invention; crip negativity as cause and effect.

In this final chapter, I want to speculate on crip negativity's dual roles as cause and effect. These entwined capacities gesture toward its methodological affordances, revealing crip negativity not only as a response to an ableist world but also as a generator of an anti-ableist something else. I opened this book with a meditation on crip negativity as method, a way of taking in the world. The first chapter explains the critical alterity of crip negativity—its capacity to thrust us into a different affective and epistemic domain from the one typically associated with the category of *disability*. As a method, crip negativity invites us to feel our bad crip feelings cripply and to think through what our bad crip feelings might tell us about the structural flaws of the world we live in, including those flaws that have emerged under the rubric of *disability*'s sociopolitical turn. The second and third chapters are more practical. We might understand them as orientational because they ask processual questions, such as, How do you get to crip negativity? What does crip negativity look like? Access thievery and life strikes are crip negative practices; they help us to assume a crip negative position. Throughout these preceding chapters, I emphasize the relationality of crip negativity. It is not a position worth holding by yourself for very long. Only when practiced in community can crip negativity manifest its full potential. Here, I pull together the preceding chapters to ask perhaps the most important question of all: What do we do once we arrive? Once a collective posture of crip negativity has been assumed, what happens next? I begin to answer this question by mapping a methodology for our bad crip feelings, by offering some initial thoughts on what crip negativity gives us, even as it indulges our refusals.

Crip negativity is intended to be an affective reprieve, a postponement or cancellation of our engagement with the world as it is. As a reprieve, crip negativity is not meant to replace any existing politic. It offers a mode of critique and a method of escape. By allowing us to acknowledge how much everything sucks, how much it hurts that everything sucks, and how much it weighs to feel like nothing is going to stop sucking anytime soon, crip negativity arms us with the strength to avoid concessions or to settle for less than we're worth. It can be easy to accept less when we feel like we're worth less, and we feel like we're worth less when we're forced into a position of gratitude for what little we already have. Crip negativity refuses gratitude, refuses generosity, refuses optimism—not because these feelings aren't good or helpful or important but because they're unsustainable and often inauthentic. Good feelings, such as pride, self-love, and hope, can be weaponized against disabled people when they're presented as affective prerequisites for our liberation. Sometimes, as Sara Ahmed explains, "activism is imagined as converting unhappy queers into happy ones" (2010, 108). The same can be said for disability activism: too often are disabled people expected to be pleased each time our basic access needs are met, as if accommodation were the pinnacle of anti-ableism.

We're expected to be happy with the bare minimum, and then our performed happiness is used to justify the bare minimum as sufficient. Yet, if we fail to appear happy, we're taken to be indignant, stubborn, or selfish for refusing to be made happy by the things that should make us happy. Ahmed, for this reason, would call us "affect aliens" (2017, 57). Affectively alienated and alienated because of our affect, "we are not made happy by the right things" (57). Bad crip feelings expose the limits of the ableist logic underpinning integrative access. If we refuse to be made happy by the access we're given, if we demand more than the bare minimum, we usher ourselves onto a new horizon of crip possibility that invites us to ask for more. Crip negativity wants us to want more, and it gives us the tools to understand just how much more it is possible for us to want.

Crip Negativity as Methodology

The tools I'm referring to are of an affective sort. Consistent with crip negativity's commitment to holding space for bad crip feelings, its tools can also be described in terms of feeling—not only our own feelings but also those of others, especially those others' feelings that reciprocally come to shape our feelings toward ourselves. My thinking on this methodology is indebted to Julie Avril Minich, whose "critical disability studies methodology" responds to a question similar to the one driving this chapter: "What do we want our work to *do*?" (2016). Minich proposes that the answer lies in the absences dotting the field of disability studies, to who and what are missing. For her, the value of a critical disability studies methodology is that it deemphasizes the category of *disability* in order to interrogate "the social norms that define particular attributes as impairments, as well as the social conditions that concentrate stigmatized attributes in particular populations." Her methodology attends to the production of *disability*, to how it is made and sustained across cultures and lines of difference.

A crip negative methodology similarly decenters the category of *disability*, but it also decenters *disability*'s analysis. Crip negativity dwells less on the norms structuring *disability* than on the processes by which the category is secured through its deferrals, through that broad category of debility that names *disability*'s excesses and residue (Puar 2017). While disability and debility often overlap—sometimes producing each other—their categorical distinction can be useful in order to emphasize the ontological violence entailed by the recuperation of *disability* into a legible social category. Crip negativity dials in on who is left behind when being disabled becomes a respectable way of being in the world.

While a critical disability studies methodology focuses on the conditions that surround *disability*, a crip negative methodology zooms out to capture the stratified formation of these conditions, alongside those that regulate or withhold the recognition of some people's illnesses, traumas, and impairments as disabilities. That is, crip negativity adopts a scalar perspective to show both the norms underpinning the category of *disability* and the norms preventing the category's democratization. I find it helpful to think about this methodological distinction through the language of affect: What feelings produce the conditions that shape *disability*? And how are these feelings tethered to forms of harm, debilitation, and violence that, through their obfuscating power, work to consolidate the category of *disability* in the moment of its emergence? By shifting toward affect, we can more easily back away from the subject of disability to chart its ontological distribution and distributed effects.

As a methodology, crip negativity encourages us to name the feelings that have historically been projected onto disability—pity, disgust, grief, anger, and resentment, to name a few—alongside those feelings that predict its liberal rehabilitation—pride, love, desire, and contentment, among others. Then, importantly, crip negativity urges us to further consider how these feelings regulate the boundaries of *disability,* as well as how they coincide or conflict with the feelings that mark its exclusions, such as indifference, apathy, hostility, and fear. These latter feelings are those that subtend others' fungibility and illegibility—feelings felt toward people living on the bad side of town, people fleeing from bad parts of the world, people rotting in confinement for doing bad things, people hurting as collateral damage in wars against bad regimes, people dying en masse for being dealt a bad hand.

Crip negativity can be about the bad feelings we bear toward a culture of detachment, toward a lack of feelings that precipitates our own bad feelings. Ableism is sometimes just a fancy word for a society that doesn't give a fuck. Crip negativity is sometimes just a fancy phrase for how it feels to never have been given a fuck about or to know the damage caused to others when no fucks are given. In this sense, a crip negative methodology can sometimes be a mode of critique, a tool for calling out the affective norms that sustain a culture of detachment and for calling in disabled and nondisabled people alike who wield the category of *disability* to silence others' bad crip feelings. This is crip negativity as a mode of accountability. Critique toward correction. Using our own bad crip feelings to reveal the conditions that cause them.

This mode of accountability notwithstanding, a crip negative methodology is not reducible to critique. Crip negativity is critical, to be sure, and can at times be called on for the purpose of critique, but crip negativity does not lend itself only to the modes of critique generally espoused under the banner of negativity. I am thinking especially of queer theory's antisocial thesis introduced in chapter

1, which risks overstating the enlivening possibilities of abjection. Lee Edelman proposes "enlarging the *inhuman*" as a practice of queer negativity intended to illuminate the violence of humanism (2004, 152). However, the desirability of inhumanity is checked by its implicit ascription to disabled, poor, and racialized people. The antisocial thesis perpetually funnels its post-structuralist critique toward a project of resignifying abjection (as "a haunting, destructive excess") rather than disavowing abjection altogether (153). Efforts to resignify or reclaim inhumanity inadvertently uphold a plasticized and plasticizing economy of humanness, wherein all variations and degrees of humanity are speciated on a sliding scale toward white cis-hetero-ablenormativity (Jackson 2020). Crip negativity, by contrast, declines to work within this project of intra-human speciation. Instead, the affective spacetimes generated by bad crip feelings make room for refusal on multiple scales, including the refusal of humanist logics and the refusal of the labor of critique.

In much the same way that crip negativity bends its critical eye reflexively toward the category of *disability* and toward *crip,* so too does it remain cognizant of the limits of critical negativity as a mode of (dis)engagement. To be clear, there's no question that sometimes critique is necessary. Critique is foundational to this book, and I remain skeptical of "postcritique" arguments that downplay the importance of critique for challenging systems of power. Critique should not be straw manned into a singular genre and then repudiated without qualification (Lee 2020). Critique can be many things, and my intention is not to flatten the nuance of any of them. When I refer to "the limits of critical negativity," I'm talking about the value of critique weighed against the value of our labor. Since the work of critique is never over—there will indeed always be more to critique—sometimes the value of a particular criticism is not worth the work of performing the critique.

Sometimes the cost to our emotional, physical, and spiritual health of explaining our bad crip feelings is too high, especially for those of us who routinely play the role of the critic. At times, this role is more or less assigned. Ahmed (2017) likens this assignation to the burden of a "feminist killjoy"—someone who feels compelled to critique injustice because no one else will do it. While critiquing injustice is certainly useful, Ahmed also reminds us to ask "how the requirement to be useful is distributed" (2019, 10). Too often are disabled people tasked with the responsibility of bringing attention to ableism, thereby transforming us into crip killjoys. A common example of this responsibility is produced by retrofit models of access, which provide accommodations only upon request and which remain standard in most institutional settings, including universities (Dolmage 2008). Forcing disabled students, staff, and faculty to secure accommodations through a disability services office, instead of allocating resources to ensure access for everyone regardless of their diagnostic status, is paramount to displacing the labor of creating access back onto those of us who don't yet have it.

The problem with this displacement is twofold. First, it absolves nondisabled people and institutions of their complicity with ableism because it allows them to ignore disabled people until explicitly instructed otherwise. Second, it demands a tremendous amount of crip labor that is not guaranteed to produce any results. Accommodations can be delayed, and requests can be outright denied. Not to mention, the labor involved in pursuing contingent access can produce "recursive debility," according to Emily Lim Rogers (2022), among those whose symptoms are exacerbated by extraneous exertion. Sometimes, the labor of critique can cause more bad crip feelings than it excises. Negativity can lead us to critique, but critique can also lead us back to negativity. Once this cycle has been established, it can be difficult to break. Negativity begetting critique begetting negativity and back again.

As if this cycle weren't concerning enough, there is another form of critique occasioned not by the absence of other critics (e.g., when you have to point out a menu's inaccessibility because no one else in your family cares to check) but by the inverse. I am referring to a mimetic logic that can make critique feel obligatory when you're surrounded by others who are being critical. Eve Kosofsky Sedgwick ascribes this mimetic logic to a kind of para-political paranoia, which "seems to require being imitated to be understood" (2002, 131). The more often a critique is made, the more important it can seem to make again. Mimesis is especially apparent on social media, where the performance of critique can be linked to the maintenance of a reputation. On Twitter, where I am active in disability, queer, trans, and academic communities, the performance of critique corresponds with the daily discourse, an ever-changing cycle of controversial tweets, articles, or events that dominate the conversation. It is not unusual to encounter dozens of nearly identical tweets all containing some variation of the same critique. In this case, critiquing the problematic object of the day—whether it's an insensitive tweet by a celebrity, a poorly vetted *New York Times* article, or a repulsive piece of anti-trans legislation—can feel coerced. The act of critique ultimately becomes not about shifting anyone's perspective about an object but about reinforcing everyone's perspective about you. This is critique for the sake of performance, not politics; or rather, critique for the sake of performing politics.

Admittedly, I am generalizing. Not all critique on social media is mimetic, and not all mimetic critique is reducible to virtue signaling. There's a cathartic quality to being critical, even if your critique isn't particularly original. Commiseration feels good. It can be a form of sharing bad crip feelings, and it can be an effective way to build crip negative communities. It is important to remember, though, that critique does not need to be the only outlet for our negativity. The reciprocal relationship between critique and bad crip feelings can make performing critique feel compulsory. Since bad crip feelings can produce the exigency for critique, it can also feel like critique is the only route to alleviating our bad crip feelings. But this circular logic is an effect only of negativity's inertia. Unless alternative vents are made available, the number of bad crip feelings will multiply through critique, not shrink.

Let's use an example. For those of us who are active in online disability communities, it can feel necessary to comment on each problematic representation of disabled people in media—each casting of a nondisabled actor to play a disabled character, each overcoming trope, each supercrip. This feeling of necessity comes from our "faith in exposure," our belief that critique will reveal the source of our bad crip feelings and, once revealed, the source of our bad crip feelings will evaporate (Sedgwick 138). But this faith is misplaced. Trusting in exposure presumes that people don't already know about the problems we're seeking to expose (141). Often, our critiques don't reveal anything new to people, such as when they're broadcast to our friends and followers online. Even when our critiques reach new audiences, making a problem visible is not always a sufficient motivator for change. The persistence of ableist casting decisions and narrative tropes, despite decades of disability criticism, would suggest that perhaps awareness isn't the only problem. In fact, sometimes exposure can make a problem worse, such as when it draws attention to a vulnerable population who is already a target for state violence (Johnson and Kennedy 2020). If a lack of exposure isn't always to blame, and if repeated critique can worsen our bad crip feelings, then perhaps critique isn't always the best use of our limited time and energy.

Fortunately, crip negativity offers more than an invitation to criticism. It operates in an alternative spacetime to paranoia that gives us a way out of the hamster wheel of critique. We might recall from chapter 1 that crip negativity runs on crip/trauma/mad time and, as such, is more concerned about holding space for bad feelings in the present than about making promises to fix the future. As a methodology, crip negativity remains an affective praxis: an expression of bad crip feelings felt crifully. This praxis invites us to sit with people and memories and texts that share in our crip feelings, rather than to position ourselves only and ever against those who do not. To "sit with" is to assume something akin to what Sedgwick calls a "reparative position" (146). In this position, paranoia is relinquished in favor of a different kind of discomfort, not the certain discomfort of negatively charged critique but the uncertain discomfort of surprise and hope. *Surprise* because you realize for the first time that you aren't alone in your bad crip feelings. *Hope* because you begin to wonder, however hesitantly, how feeling bad and feeling crip with someone else might change your feelings entirely.

Typically, hope is cataloged as a good feeling. Crip negativity rightfully leads us to be suspicious of good feelings. It's no secret that hope has been known to function as tool for placation and avoidance. In its purest form, though, to hope is merely "to entertain expectation of something desired" (*OED Online* 2022). Hope can be a good feeling, but it's also and always contiguous with bad feelings because it emerges from lack, from want, and from need. Hope does not require confidence or assurance; it is not faith. Hope is openness to the possibility of the unknown, a willingness "to entertain expectation." When felt in community, hope—along with surprise—is part of what differentiates crip negativity from other variations of critical negativity. Hope suspends crips, however slightly, above the floor of resignation. It keeps us alert and attentive. It reminds us that our bad crip feelings are worth feeling because they, in turn, remind us of what we're worth. Hope gives crips a structure for our negativity. One that demands no recognition, no gratitude—only a promise not to dissolve into the abyss of our pain.

In this context, a reparative position does not deny the affective intensity of crip negativity. It is not meant to replace bad crip feelings with good crip feelings. The reparative, to be clear, is not rehabilitative. Unlike Anna Mollow's (2012) "rehabilitative futurism," the reparative does not attempt to cure our bad crip feelings or to realign their expression with able-normative expectations for "healthy" and "appropriate" emotional responses. Crip negativity coexists with the reparative because they are both "additive and accretive" (Sedgwick 149). When practiced reparatively, crip negativity gels through the deep affective connections established across crip negative differences—across the range of identities, positionalities, and community affiliations that bear their own bad crip feelings. I don't need to convince you to see the world like I do because I don't believe that seeing the world particularly offers any guarantee that the world will change particularly. I do believe, however, in urging you to feel deeply about the world, to attend to others' feelings about the world, and to map how our differential feelings inform the ways we treat one another. Perhaps by feeling this jumble of feelings together, we won't feel so alone when we eventually return to the work of changing the world for the better.

Changing the world for the better, after all, remains the ultimate goal. Despite that crip negativity is itself a practice of refusal, including a refusal of the labor of liberation, it is also a practice meant to be taken up in the context of that labor. Meaning: crip negativity is not a permanent bowing out, not a totalizing disavowal, not an isolating position. There is an ethics to crip negativity, to how and for what purpose we indulge our bad crip feelings. Our feelings are our own, and in an ideal world, we'd be able to feel them whenever, wherever, however, and for however long we want. But given the stratification of humanity under liberalism, feelings cannot be disarticulated from power. As such, the expression of bad crip feelings must sometimes be negotiated among crips who all have bad feelings in need of expression. At the end of the day, what matters is our shared commitment to the right of expression and our mutual acknowledgement that one person's expression can impact the conditions of another's. Minich reminds us that "the ethical value (or lack thereof) in a disability studies methodology will lie in the form that methodology takes" (2017). The same holds true for a crip negative methodology, which gleans its ethicality from the purposes for which we use it.

Crip negativity is meant for those who have historically been denied the freedom to indulge their bad crip feelings, for those whose forms of crip expression are policed and disciplined, and for those whose bad crip feelings are sidelined by the persistent focus on the feelings of those who more closely approximate normativity. To feel bad crip feelings cripply includes being aware of *crip*'s contingencies, that is, to feel *crip* cripply by attending to the power dynamics that determine whose feelings deserve our attention and when. Sorting through the mess of bad crip feelings in community with other crips is where the ethical value of crip negativity lies. It's the *sitting with* that makes crip negativity worthwhile. Crip negativity does not orient us toward the future or toward justice or toward measurable, material change, but it does allocate us a spacetime to collectively mourn how much change is needed. We can't change the world for the better until we allow ourselves to feel the depth of our grief. It is only from those depths—dug further still from the multiplicative effect of crip negative communion—that we can even begin to know what change is needed. Crip negativity jars us loose from the world as we know it, so that later on we can more conscientiously articulate the world as we want it.

Sitting with Crip Negativity

In the spirit of sitting with others' crip negativity, I want to end by placing one of the awkward poems I wrote in high school into conversation with two other poems—each by an acclaimed poet with whom I have had the pleasure of sharing bad crip feelings. Both of these poets know what it's like to be overcome by negativity, to be held in its grip, as well as what it feels like to bear that negativity all alone. Their poems, though far superior to my own, carry with them similar scars. I often seek out the work of Travis Chi Wing Lau and Cameron Awkward-Rich to remind me that I am not the only one who feels bad crip feelings. In this final section, I return to their work once again to read their negativity alongside my own.

A part of me does not want to share my old poetry because I am embarrassed by it—no, because I'm embarrassed by the boy who wrote it. I want to love Awkward John; he is me, after all. But after all these years, I still harbor so much pain toward the life that scared boy lived. This pain takes shape as resentment and disgust at the boy himself. (Truthfully, I am shaking as I write these sentences.) I am so ashamed. I wish I didn't hate the child I once was because that child doesn't deserve hate, because I am that child, because Awkward Logan doesn't deserve hate. But I do hate him. I do hate me. I do. I'm so sorry. I—

Breathe. One moment. Bad crip feelings being felt cripply.

Hate, like love, is a practice, not a position.

In an effort to turn my own crip negativity inward, toward the way that ableism lingers in the bad feelings I bear toward myself, I need to share with you who that self once was and maybe still is—in all his/their fragile, earnest, frightened, yearning glory. The poem is fittingly, awkwardly titled "Life on Earth," and it begins like this:

To live

To lie

To live to lie

To lie to live

We all will die

But until that time I cry

To the ones that ignore and pass me by

My desperate calls are all in vain

As my sins have covered what's been slain

For I know the Words that speak the truth

But I know my heart is forever doomed

I would attempt to rise up and stand

But reason calls and reason lands

Why try when hope is lost

Why live when lies are what it costs

To survive in a world where love is lust

And people are only dirt and dust

Reading these stanzas is difficult for me. I feel so deeply the force of the bad feelings that my young self felt. I believed myself to be a fraud because performing cisheteronormativity and neurotypicality felt like lying. My whole life was spent lying, so lying was the only way I knew how to live. It was not just that I struggled to embrace myself but that I could not even fathom the softness that such an embrace would provide. I felt ignored, passed by, doomed, and lost. Not even the Bible, which I held fast against my chest before bed, could reassure me. I was a child who had yet to live but was already prepared to die.

The lines that stand out most to me are the ones that speak to why I was so despondent: "I would attempt to rise up and stand / But reason calls and reason lands." Reason. A word I thought meant truth but have since come to realize is just what others expect you to endure. A core tenet of Enlightenment thinking, Reason is at the foundation of liberal humanism, taking credit for all it promises and justifying all it withholds. Reason is freedom, autonomy, liberty, and independence, alongside homophobia, cissexism, racism, and ableism. Reason is a Southern Baptist church, an abusive home, a school filled with bullies. Reason purports to jettison feelings in favor of objectivity but, in the process, excises all of us with feelings toward Reason itself.

Awkward John may not have had the words to share his feelings about what Reason was doing to him, how it was fueling his pain and teaching him to turn his bad feelings against himself. But Awkward Logan does have the words, at least some of them, and I am grateful to be in community with others who have more and better words than I do. Words that name hurt and story injury. Lau's poem "Pithy" and Awkward-Rich's "Essay on the Awkward / Black / Object" are built with these words. Both have helped me to mine the depths of my own negativity, and they've also taken me to new depths, burrowing into dark places I'd never known before. From these depths and dark places, I've learned to feel the world differently—in much the same way I hope this book helps you to feel the world differently too. We're compiling an archive of bad crip feelings, all of us, which is another way of saying we're building a world on crip/trauma/mad time. We're feeling together—now and later, here and there—shoveling our way toward a core of pain that many of us have spent our lifetimes avoiding. We're getting there, though: incrementally, collectively, and cripply.

In his book *Paring* (2018), Lau paints a world of pain; or at least, a world as it is experienced by a bodymind in perpetual pain. Toward the end of the collection, "Pithy" serves as the clearest articulation of that painful world's core. The piece comprises fifteen enumerated stanzas, each including a refrain set off by the word "pith," for terse and tissue. The poem begins,

> 1. I shrug off my messenger onto the floor and forget to kiss you when I walk through the door.
>
> *Pith: the pain has its steel hoop around my lumbar.*
>
> 2. I catch myself tottering—a deformation of my walk.
>
> *Pith: a family resemblance: the curvature progresses faster than any other before me. I am not yet thirty.* (23)

While the initial line of each stanza describes what is observable about the speaker's experience of disability—the movements, postures, and lapses that accompany a body in pain—the refrain captures the invisible context boiling the speaker's negativity beneath their surface.

Bad crip feelings seethe alongside the physicality of disability as unspoken thoughts and fears and fantasies. They are connected, inseparable even, from the experience of living in a particular body, and yet they are stoked by the conditions that surround it. "3. I take a tumble after I miss the curb," Lau writes. "*Pith: had you not caught me by the arm, I would have finally broken my first bone*" (23). The speaker is in pain because their body feels like its breaking, but their negativity is fueled by the ableism of a world from which they find themselves breaking away. A world where clarity of thought and speech determines a person's respectability: "8. I cannot form sentences. Non-sequitur, organic hesitancy. / *Pith: I would never wish upon anyone a life in the thickness of fog. The shame of being lost in it*" (23). A world where dependence is something to fear: "9. I can't make it up the stairs while cradling the box. / *Pith: I hate admitting that I will have to depend on you more and more. That you will have to lie to me that it's okay*" (23). A world where labor defines who you are: "I look perpetually exhausted. / *Pith: pain redefines what labor means*" (23). The pith in this poem is the crip negativity burning through the speaker's veins against Reason. It's the same negativity that hums a low note to all of us crips, eating away at our meat, as we watch the world go on from our windows and from the other side of our screens—the one that buzzes our crip feelings louder and louder until they rattle our scorched bones, and we feel like we might die.

But we don't die, usually. Instead, we learn that there's something rather astonishing about feeling as cripply—as intensely—as we do. There's a power laden in our negativity that emerges all on its own if we let it. We don't need to find our power. We just need to let it flow. For Awkward-Rich, the power of bad crip feelings emanates from the interstice of awkwardness and Blackness. In "Essay on the Awkward / Black / Object," which appears in *Sympathetic Little Monster* (2018), Awkward-Rich meditates on the racialization of "awkward," which is both the speaker's father's last name and, for the speaker, a mode of Black being. While awkwardness is not a diagnostic category, its adjectival form allegorizes disability, in much the same way that my peers heralded my neurodivergence by calling me Awkward John. As a racialized term, "awkward" reveals the contingence and tension between race and disability: at once overlapping and yet cleaved apart. Reflecting on the history of slavery through which many African Americans received their last names, Awkward-Rich writes, "You already know the story. A man is made into a thing & sutured to it. The name" (18). The name "Awkward" recalls a violent, familial history but also gestures toward an escape from it, a flight from its inheritance: "*Awkward* as both punishment & method" (23). As method, awkwardness is a form of negativity and refusal. It is, at once, a recognition of the status of Blackness in an antiblack world—"As long as the object works it is bound to its own annihilation" (21)—and a resignification of that status. "The solution?" the poem's speaker tells us plainly, "Fall. Fall apart. Decay" (21). To fall apart and decay is to allow the wash of negativity to soak you through. It's to breathe with the chill of your skin as the negativity dries. To adopt such affective stillness, to be held fast in the iciness of bad crip feelings, is to embrace the power of refusal.

This isn't the reclaimed power of the category of *disability*, a power bestowed by legibility. This isn't really empowerment at all. This power is sourced internally by refusing Reason. It's to refuse the expectation of endurance. It's to refuse your own instrumentalization—as disabled, as racialized, as queer. Not because you aren't those things but because you aren't those things in the way they want you to be. They as family, as employer, as school, as government, as society, as capitalism, as ableism, as white supremacy, as cisheterosexism. To fall. Fall apart. Decay. These things we can do. We do them so very well. So well, in fact, we might call them symptomatic of a debility drive: not ushered into death or disability—contra Edelman and Mollow—but receding back into debility, into fungibility, into the obscurity of invisibility that comes with refusing categorical adherence. This is not a romanticization of abjection nor a negligent omission of people who never had access to the category of *disability* to begin with; rather, it is a condition of abolition for us all. It's here in the dark that we can breathe deepest, not because the air is particularly clean, but because there's no reason to be embarrassed if we cough, choke, or slobber on ourselves. It's here in the dark that we find one another, each groping our way through our bad feelings. And upon our fingers' first contact, we break down completely. Because now we can, at last. Because it feels so good to feel this bad with one arm under your neck, another around your waist, and my knees cupped behind your legs: awkward and crippled and together.

Bibliography

Ahmed, Sara. 2010. *The Promise of Happiness*. Durham, N.C.: Duke University Press.

Ahmed, Sara. 2017. *Living a Feminist Life*. Durham, N.C.: Duke University Press.

Ahmed, Sara. 2019. *What's the Use? On the Uses of Use*. Durham, N.C.: Duke University Press.

Aho, Tanja N. 2017. "Active Citizenship, Liberalism, and Labor-Normativity: Queercrip Resistance, Sanist Anxiety, and Racialized Ableism in Viewer Responses to *Here Comes Honey Boo Boo*." *Journal of Literary and Cultural Disability Studies* 11 (3): 321–37.

Amin, Kadji. 2017. *Disturbing Attachments: Genet, Modern Pederasty, and Queer History*. Durham, N.C.: Duke University Press.

Awkward-Rich, Cameron. 2016. *Sympathetic Little Monster*. Los Angeles: Ricochet Editions.

babylon, femi. 2019. "Defined/Definers: My Thoughts on Common Terminology around Erotic Labor and Trafficking." *Medium*, September 9, 2019. https://medium.com/heauxthots/heauxthots-defined-definers-my-thoughts-on-common-terminology-around-erotic-labor-trafficking-f9df45ea2b9a.

babylon, femi, and Heather Berg. 2021. "Erotic Labor within and without Work: An Interview with femi babylon." *South Atlantic Quarterly* 120 (3): 631–40.

Bailey, Courtney. 2019. "On the Impossible: Disability Studies, Queer Theory, and the Surviving Crip." *Disability Studies Quarterly* 39 (4). https://doi.org/10.18061/dsq.v39i4.6580.

Bearden, Elizabeth B. 2019. *Monstrous Kinds: Body, Space, and Narrative in Renaissance Representations of Disability*. Ann Arbor: University of Michigan Press.

Bell, Chris. 2006. "Introducing White Disability Studies: A Modest Proposal." In *The Disability Studies Reader*, edited by Lennard J. Davis, 275–82. New York: Routledge.

Ben-Moshe, Liat. 2020. *Decarcerating Disability: Deinstitutionalization and Prison Abolition*. Minneapolis: University of Minnesota Press.

Berlant, Lauren. 2011. *Cruel Optimism*. Durham, N.C.: Duke University Press.

Bersani, Leo. 1995. *Homos*. Cambridge, Mass.: Harvard University Press.

Bey, Marquis. 2017. "The Trans*-ness of Blackness, the Blackness of Trans*-ness." *Transgender Studies Quarterly* 4 (2): 275–95.

Bruce, La Marr Jurelle. 2016. "The Body Beautiful: Black Drag, American Cinema, and the Heteroperpetually Ever After." In *No Tea, No Shade: New Writings in Black Queer Studies*, edited by E. Patrick Johnson, 166–95. Durham, N.C.: Duke University Press.

Bruce, La Marr Jurelle. 2021. *How to Go Mad without Losing Your Mind: Madness and Black Radical Creativity*. Durham, N.C.: Duke University Press.

Caprariello, Alex, and Russell Falcon. 2021. "14 Children with Disabilities File First Federal Lawsuit against Gov. Abbott over Mask Mandate Ban." *KTAL*, August 18, 2021. https://www.arklatexhomepage.com /news/state-news/texas/14-children-with-disabilities-file-first-federal -lawsuit-against-gov-abbott-over-mask-mandate-ban/.

Carlisle, Vanessa. 2021. "'Sex Work Is Star Shaped': Antiwork Politics and the Value of Embodied Knowledge." *South Atlantic Quarterly* 120 (3): 573–90.

Caserio, Robert L., Lee Edelman, Jack Halberstam, José Esteban Muñoz, and Tim Dean. 2006. "The Antisocial Thesis in Queer Theory." *PMLA* 121 (3): 819–28.

Cedillo, Christina, and M. Remi Yergeau. 2019. "Workshop 7: Crip Is a Verb." *Rhetoric Society of America*, 2019. https://www.rhetoricsociety .org/aws/RSA/pt/sd/news_article/171978/_blank/layout_details/false.

Courtney-Long, Elizabeth A., Sebastian D. Romano, Dianna D. Carroll, and Michael H. Fox. 2017. "Socioeconomic Factors at the Intersection of Race and Ethnicity Influencing Health Risks for People with Disabilities." *Journal of Racial and Ethnic Health Disparities* 4:213–22.

Crosby, Christina, and Janet R. Jakobsen. 2020. "Disability, Debility, and Caring Queerly." *Social Text* 38 (4): 77–103.

Dallas Morning News. 2013. "Texas Gov. Greg Abbott Has Received $7.8 Million from Suit over Accident That Disabled Him." August 2, 2013. https://www.dallasnews.com/news/politics/2013/08/03/greg-abbott -has-received-6-million-from-suit-over-accident-that-disabled-him/.

Dallas Morning News. 2014. "Greg Abbott Pushes to Block Disabled Texans' Lawsuits against State." February 15, 2014. https://www .dallasnews.com/news/politics/2014/02/16/greg-abbott-pushes-to -block-disabled-texans-lawsuits-against-state/.

Dey, Sneha, and Karen Brooks Harper. 2022. "Transgender Texas Kids Are Terrified after Governor Orders That Parents Be Investigated

for Child Abuse." *Texas Tribune*, February 28, 2022. https://www
.texastribune.org/2022/02/28/texas-transgender-child-abuse/.

Dilts, Andrew. 2012. "Incurable Blackness: Criminal Disenfranchisement, Mental Disability, and the White Citizen." *Disability Studies Quarterly* 32 (3). https://doi.org/10.18061/dsq.v32i3.3268.

Dolmage, Jay. 2008. "Mapping Composition: Inviting Disability in the Front Door." In *Disability and Teaching of Writing*, edited by Cynthia Lewiecki-Wilson and Brenda Jo Brueggemann, 14–27. Boston: Bedford / St. Martin's Press.

Dolmage, Jay. 2014. *Disability Rhetoric*. Syracuse, N.Y.: Syracuse University Press.

Dolmage, Jay. 2018. *Disabled upon Arrival: Eugenics, Immigration, and the Construction of Race and Disability*. Columbus: Ohio State University Press.

Edelman, Lee. 2004. *No Future: Queer Theory and the Death Drive*. Durham, N.C.: Duke University Press.

Edelman, Lee. 2007. "Ever After: History, Negativity, and the Social." *South Atlantic Quarterly* 106 (3): 469–76.

Erevelles, Nirmala. 2002. "(Im)material Citizens: Cognitive Disability, Race, and the Politics of Citizenship." *Disability, Culture, and Education* 1 (1): 5–25.

Erevelles, Nirmala. 2011. *Disability and Difference in Global Contexts: Enabling a Transformative Body Politic*. New York: Palgrave Macmillan.

Erevelles, Nirmala. 2014. "Thinking with Disability Studies." *Disability Studies Quarterly* 34 (2). https://doi.org/10.18061/dsq.v34i2.4248.

Erevelles, Nirmala, and Andrea Minear. 2010. "Unspeakable Offenses: Untangling Race and Disability in Discourses of Intersectionality." *Journal of Literary and Cultural Disability Studies* 4 (2): 127–45.

Erkulwater, Jennifer L. 2018. "How the Nation's Largest Minority Became White: Race Politics and the Disability Rights Movement, 1970–1980." *Journal of Policy History* 30 (3): 367–99.

Forrest, Brady James. 2020. "Crip Feelings/Feeling Crip." *Journal of Literary and Cultural Disability Studies* 14 (1): 75–89.

Franzino, Jean. 2016. "Lewis Clarke and the 'Color' of Disability: The Past and Future of Black Disability Studies." *Disability Studies Quarterly* 36 (4). https://doi.org/10.18061/dsq.v36i4.

Garland-Thomson, Rosemarie. 2011. "Misfits: A Feminist Materialist Disability Concept." *Hypatia: A Journal of Feminist Philosophy* 26 (3): 591–609.

Gill, Michael. 2015. *Already Doing It: Intellectual Disability and Sexual Agency*. Minneapolis: University of Minnesota Press.

Halberstam, Jack. 2013. "The Wild Beyond: With and for the Undercommons." In *The Undercommons: Fugitive Planning and Black Study*, by Stefano Harney and Fred Moten, 2–13. New York: Minor Compositions.

Hamraie, Aimi. 2017. *Building Access: Universal Design and the Politics of Disability.* Minneapolis: University of Minnesota Press.

Harney, Stefano, and Fred Moten. 2013. *The Undercommons: Fugitive Planning and Black Study.* New York: Minor Compositions.

Hartman, Saidiya V. 1997. *Scenes of Subjection: Terror, Slavery, and Self-Making in Nineteenth-Century America.* New York: Oxford University Press.

Henderson, Taylor. 2019. "Ryan O'Connell Hopes to Destigmatize Gay Sex with Netflix's *Special.*" *Pride,* April 11, 2019. https://www.pride.com /tv/2019/4/11/ryan-oconnell-hopes-destigmatize-gay-sex-netflixs -special.

Hersey, Tricia. 2020a. "Interconnectedness and Liberation." *Nap Ministry,* January 2, 2020. https://thenapministry.wordpress.com/2020/01/02 /interconnectedness-and-liberation/.

Hersey, Tricia. 2020b. "Resources for the Rest Resistance. This Is about More Than Naps." *Nap Ministry,* January 17, 2020. https:// thenapministry.wordpress.com/2020/01/17/resources-for-the-rest -resistance-this-is-about-more-than-naps/.

Hersey, Tricia. 2021. "Our Work Has a Framework: REST IS RESISTANCE." *Nap Ministry,* January 11, 2021. https://thenapministry.wordpress.com /2021/01/11/our-work-is-has-a-framework/.

Hubbard, Kaia. 2021. "Few States Require LGBTQ-Inclusive Sex Education, Report Finds." *U.S. News and World Report,* May 26, 2021. https://www.usnews.com/news/best-states/articles/2021-05-26/few -states-require-lgbtq-inclusive-sex-education.

Jackson, Zakiyyah Iman. 2020. *Becoming Human: Matter and Meaning in an Antiblack World.* New York: New York University Press.

Jade, Hayley. 2021a. "I'm an Autistic Sex Worker, and Here's Why It Works for Me." *HuffPost,* April 30, 2021. https://www.huffpost.com /entry/autistic-sex-worker-masking_n_608a343ce4b02e74d2233bfa.

Jade, Hayley. 2021b. "I'm a Disabled Escort Living with Chronic Illness. Here's Why I Love My Job." *Uncomfortable Revolution,* https://www .urevolution.com/disabled-sex-worker-with-a-chronic-illness/.

Johnson, Jenell, and Krista Kennedy. 2020. "Introduction: Disability, In/ visibility, and Risk." *Rhetoric Society Quarterly* 50 (3): 161– 65.

Kafer, Alison. 2013. *Feminist, Queer, Crip.* Bloomington: Indiana University Press.

Kafer, Alison. 2017. "Health Rebels: A Crip Manifesto on Social Justice." *YouTube,* April 6, 2017. https://www.youtube.com/watch?v= YqcOUD1pBKw.

Kim, Jina B. 2021. "Cripping the Welfare Queen: The Radical Potential of Disability Politics." *Social Text* 39 (3): 79–101.

Kirst, Seamus. 2019. "'Special' Creator Ryan O'Connell Wants to 'Make Gay Sh*t for Gay People.'" *Teen Vogue,* April 12, 2019. https://www .teenvogue.com/story/special-netflix-ryan-o-connell.

Kumar, Arun, Deepa Sonpal, and Vanmala Hiranandani. 2012. "Trapped between Ableism and Neoliberalism: Critical Reflections on Disability and Employment in India." *Disability Studies Quarterly* 32 (3). https://dsq-sds.org/index.php/dsq/article/view/3235/3109.

Lau, Travis Chi Wing. 2020. *Paring.* Georgetown, Ky.: Finishing Line Press.

Lee, Nathan. 2020. "Postcritique and the Form of the Question: *Whose Critique Has Run Out of Steam?*" *Cultural Critique* 108:150–76.

Lee, Sean. 2019. "Crip Horizons: Disability Art Futurism." *Akimbo,* September 25, 2019. https://akimbo.ca/akimblog/crip-horizons -disability-art-futurism-by-sean-lee/.

Lopez, Brian. 2021. "GOP Bill Targeting How Race, Slavery, and History Are Taught in Texas Schools Heads to Gov. Greg Abbott's Desk." *Texas Tribune,* September 2, 2021. https://www.texastribune.org/2021/09/02 /texas-race-history-schools/.

Lukin, Josh. 2013. "Disability and Blackness." In *The Disability Studies Reader,* edited by Lennard J. Davis, 308–15: New York: Routledge.

Malatino, Hil. 2019. *Queer Embodiment: Monstrosity, Medical Violence, and Intersex Experience.* Lincoln: University of Nebraska Press.

McCullough, Jolie. 2021. "Migrants Arrested by Texas in Border Crackdown Are Being Imprisoned for Weeks without Legal Help or Formal Charges." *Texas Tribune,* September 27, 2021. https://www .texastribune.org/2021/09/27/texas-border-migrants-jail/.

McRuer, Robert. 2006. *Crip Theory: Cultural Signs of Queerness and Disability.* New York: New York.

Mekelburg, Madlin. 2022. "Supreme Court Overturns Roe v. Wade, Trigger Law to Completely Ban Abortion in Texas." *Austin American-Statesman,* June 24, 2022. https://www.statesman.com/story/news /politics/state/2022/06/24/roe-v-wade-abortion-texas-supreme-court -decision/7528731001/.

Mingus, Mia. 2017. "Access Intimacy, Interdependence and Disability Justice." *Leaving Evidence,* April 12, 2017. https://leavingevidence .wordpress.com/2017/04/12/access-intimacy-interdependence-and -disability-justice/.

Minich, Julie Avril. 2016. "Enabling Whom? Critical Disability Studies Now." *Lateral* 5 (1). http://www.doi.org/10.25158/L5.1.9.

Minich, Julie Avril. 2017. "Thinking with Jina B. Kim and Sami Schalk." *Lateral* 6 (1). https://doi.org/10.25158/l6.1.15.

Miranda, Gabriela. 2022. "'Dream come true': Puerto Rican Model Is Victoria's Secret First With Down Syndrome." *USA Today,* February 17, 2022. https://www.usatoday.com/story/entertainment/celebrities /2022/02/17/victorias-secret-model-down-syndrome/6827199001/.

Mollow, Anna. 2012. "Is Sex Disability? Queer Theory and the Disability Drive." In *Sex and Disability,* edited by Robert McRuer and Anna Mollow, 285–312. Durham, N.C.: Duke University Press.

Moon, Zia. 2018. "As a Sex Worker with a Chronic Illness, FOSTA Means Losing My Medical Care." *Vice*, June 18, 2018. https://www.vice.com /en/article/xwm5pd/sex-work-chronic-illness-disability-fosta-v25n2.

Morrigan, Clementine. 2017. "Trauma Time: The Queer Temporalities of the Traumatized Mind." *Somatechnics* 7 (1): 50–58.

Muñoz, José Esteban. 2009. *Cruising Utopia: The Then and There of Queer Futurity*. New York: New York University Press.

Nunokawa, Jeff. 2007. "Queer Theory: Postmortem." *South Atlantic Quarterly* 106 (3): 553–63.

OED Online. 2022. "hope, *v.*" Oxford University Press, September 2022. http://www.oed.com/view/Entry/88372.

Osorio, Ruth. 2022. "Disabling Citizenship: Rhetorical Practices of Disabled World-Making at the 1977 504 Sit-In." *College English* 84 (1): 243–65.

Owen, Randall, and Sarah Parker Harris. 2012. "'No Rights without Responsibilities': Disability Rights and Neoliberal Reform under New Labour." *Disability Studies Quarterly* 32 (3). https://www.doi.org/10 .18061/dsq.v32i3.3283.

Owens, Deirdre Cooper. 2018. *Medical Bondage: Race, Gender, and the Origins of America Gynecology*. Athens: University of Georgia Press.

Pickens, Therí Alyce. 2019. *Black Madness: Mad Blackness*. Durham, N.C.: Duke University Press.

Piepzna-Samarasinha, Leah Lakshmi. 2018. *Care Work: Dreaming Disability Justice*. Vancouver: Arsenal Pulp.

Puar, Jasbir K. 2017. *The Right to Maim: Debility, Capacity, Disability*. Durham, N.C.: Duke University Press.

Ralph, Laurence. 2012. "What Wounds Enable: The Politics of Disability and Violence in Chicago." *Disability Studies Quarterly* 32 (3). https://doi .org/10.18061/dsq.v32i3.3270.

Rogers, Emily Lim. 2022. "Recursive Debility: Symptoms, Patient Activism, and the Incomplete Medicalization of ME/CFS." *Medical Anthropology Quarterly* 36 (3). https://doi.org/10.1111/maq.12701.

Russell, Emily. 2011. *Reading Embodied Citizenship: Disability Narrative, and the Body Politic*. New Brunswick, N.J.: Rutgers University Press.

Russell, Marta, and Ravi Malhotra. 2009. "Capitalism and Disability." *Socialist Register* 38. https://socialistregister.com/index.php/srv /article/view/5784.

Ryan, Patrick. 2019. "'Special' Creator on Show's Gay, Disabled Sex: 'People don't acknowledge we're sexual beings'." *USA Today*, April 12, 2019. https://www.usatoday.com/story/life/tv/2019/04/12/netflix -special-gay-disabled-sex-humanity-respect/3434438002/.

Sainato, Michael. 2020. "'Profit over death': Millions of American Diabetics Struggle to Afford Insulin." *The Guardian*, October 30, 2020. https://www.theguardian.com/society/2020/oct/30/americans -diabetes-insulin-cost.

Samuels, Ellen. 2017. "Six Ways of Looking at Crip Time." *Disability Studies Quarterly* 37 (3). https://doi.org/10.18061/dsq.v37i3.5824.

Sandahl, Carrie. 2003. "Queering the Crip or Cripping the Queer? Intersections of Queer and Crip Identities in Solo Autobiographical Performance." *GLQ* 9 (1–2): 25–56.

Schalk, Sami. 2013. "Coming to Claim Crip: Disidentification with/in Disability Studies." *Disability Studies Quarterly* 33 (2). https://doi.org /10.18061/dsq.v33i2.3705.

Schalk, Sami. 2017. "Critical Disability Studies as Methodology." *Lateral* 6 (1). https://doi.org/10.25158/L6.1.13.

Schalk, Sami. 2018. *Bodyminds Reimagined: (Dis)ability, Race, and Gender in Black Women's Speculative Fiction*. Durham, N.C.: Duke University Press.

Schalk, Sami. 2022. *Black Disability Politics*. Durham, N.C.: Duke University Press.

Sedgwick, Eve Kosofsky. 2002. *Touching Feeling*. Durham, N.C.: Duke University Press.

Selyukh, Alina. 2020. "Workers with Disabilities Can Earn Just $3.34 an Hour. Agency Says Law Needs Change." *NPR,* September 17, 2020. https://www.npr.org/2020/09/17/912840482/u-s-agency-urges-end-to -below-minimum-wage-for-workers-with-disabilities.

Shakespeare, Tom. 2006. "The Social Model of Disability." In *The Disability Studies Reader,* edited by Lennard J. Davis, 197–204. New York: Routledge.

Shepherd, Katie. 2021. "Rick Perry Says Texans Would Accept Even Longer Power Outages 'To Keep the Federal Government out of Their Business.'" *Washington Post,* February 18, 2021. https://www .washingtonpost.com/nation/2021/02/17/texas-abbott-wind-turbines -outages/.

Siebers, Tobin. 2012. "A Sexual Culture for Disabled People." In *Sex and Disability,* edited by Robert McRuer and Anna Mollow, 285–312. Durham, N.C.: Duke University Press.

Sins Invalid. 2015. "10 Principles of Disability Justice." September 17, 2015. https://www.sinsinvalid.org/blog/10-principles-of-disability-justice.

Smilges, J. Logan. 2022. *Queer Silence: On Disability and Rhetorical Absence*. Minneapolis: University of Minnesota Press.

Snyder, Sharon L., and David T. Mitchell. 2005. *Cultural Locations of Disability*. Chicago: University of Chicago Press.

Talbot, Hayley, Gemma DiCasimirro, and Zoë Richards. 2022. "Texas Gov. Greg Abbott to Skip NRA Convention, Return to Uvalde, Instead." *NBC News,* May 26, 2022. https://www.nbcnews.com/politics/politics-news /texas-gov-greg-abbott-skip-nra-convention-return-uvalde-instead -rcna30800.

Taylor, Sunaura. 2004. "The Right Not to Work: Power and Disability." *Monthly Review* 55 (10). https://doi.org/10.14452/MR-055-10-2004-03_2.

Tyler, Dennis. 2022 *Disabilities of the Color Line*. New York: New York University Press.

Warren, Calvin L. 2018. *Ontological Terror: Blackness, Nihilism, and Emancipation*. Durham, N.C.: Duke University Press.

Weeks, Kathi. 2011. *The Problem with Work: Feminism, Marxism, Antiwork Politics, and Postwork Imaginaries*. Durham, N.C.: Duke University Press.

Weill-Greenberg, Elizabeth. 2021. "Disabled and Abandoned in New York State Prisons." *The Nation*, October 25, 2021. https://www.thenation.com/article/society/prisons-disability-new-york/.

(Continued from page iii)

Forerunners: Ideas First

J. Logan Smilges is assistant professor of English language and literatures at the University of British Columbia and the author of *Queer Silence: On Disability and Rhetorical Absence* (Minnesota, 2022).